World History

World History
A True Story

Tom Malone

Denver, Colorado · 2019

Library of Congress Control Number: 2019911435
ISBN-13: 978-1-945236-14-3
ISBN-10: 1-945236-14-0

Printed in the United States of America
First edition, 2019

Published by Thomas R. Malone · Denver, Colorado

To the Future:

For giving us hope that you can learn from history to make the world a better place.

"Those who cannot remember the past are condemned to repeat it."

– George Santayana

Reason in Common Sense, 1905

CONTENTS

Introduction   1

Part 1: Ancient Civilizations

1. Ancient Sumer   11

2. Ancient Egypt   17

3. Indus River Valley   22

4. Aboriginal Australia   27

Part 2: Classical Civilizations

5. Ancient Greece   33

6. Roman Republic   38

7. Roman Empire 44

8. Han China 50

Part 3: Trade and Cultural Diffusion

9. Silk Road 59

10. Mali Empire 65

11. Great Zimbabwe 70

Part 4: Civilizations Collide

12. Medieval Europe 77

13. Middle Eastern Caliphates 82

14. Mongol Empire 88

15. Feudal Japan 94

Part 5: Old World vs. New World

16. Maya Empire 101

17. Incan Empire 105

18. Aztec Empire 111

19. European Renaissance 116

20. Columbian Exchange 123

Part 6: The Modern World

21. European Imperialism   131

22. World War I   138

23. World War II   144

24. Modern Globalization   151

Conclusion   159

Select Bibliography   171

Acknowledgements   183

About the Author   187

Other Works   189

INTRODUCTION

History is the story of the world. It's a story complete with compelling characters, exotic locations, plot twists, and dramatic showdowns between heroes and villains. And it's not over; the story of the world continues to develop as time moves forward. Today's current events become tomorrow's history, adding to the drama of the world's story.

The story of the world is also told through multiple narrators, which makes it even more captivating. Each person that has walked through this world has left a mark on the world's story. Some stories have been pushed to the forefront of the narrative; these tend to be famous political leaders and innovators who made decisions that have dramatically shifted humanity's direction. Then, there are the billions of human stories that have grown dusty on the shelves. These stories, the ones told by common peasants, average citizens, and forgotten heroes, have fallen into obscurity; either their stories were never recorded, forgotten in verbal traditions, or lost to the destruction of time. However, sometimes these stories do find a revival, and it tends to be the stories of average citizens that are the most compelling to modern historians.

As a student of history, I have always found the stories of famous heroes to be exciting, but the narratives of common people keep me coming back to familiar eras of history because I can always learn more. As a history teacher, I try to convey these stories to students as a means to give them multiple lenses into the past. Through multiple narrators, students can create a more complete view of an era, and they can build an understanding of a situation through empathy with more than one group of historical people.

But history isn't just the story of the past; history has shaped what we're doing right now. Your daily life is influenced by inventions that have shaped the path of human history. The wheel, the book, the engine, the compass, chess, and even the internet. Our government leaders and social norms trace their lineage back to the beginnings of civilization; customs that we consider normal today were created somewhere along the historical timeline; they carried their way through time and into our lives. And this is just part of the story.

Telling the entire story of human history is impossible. There are too many people, perspectives, events, places, and events for one person to tell an accurate, complete history of the world. By no means is this work meant to tell the complete story of history. People spend their entire lives dedicated to studying and researching one single era of history, earning doctorate degrees through which they still research, uncover, and redefine their given era of expertise. What we can do, though, is try. We can develop a basic understanding of world history's framework, and we can use the research and discoveries of expert historians to continually develop our understanding of how civilizations, eras, cultures, and people are connected through time. As individuals, we will never reach a moment where we fully understand history and can then move on to other pursuits; history is ever-changing, as it continues to become reinterpreted by these experts. It's up to us to cultivate and maintain our own understanding throughout our lives, as with any form of learning.

This work is a brief history of the world. Brief. This work is meant to give us a basic overview of the history of the world by looking at the major cultures that have shaped its development over time in hopes of inspiring future historians to learn as much as they can about as many cultures as possible. By no means does this work dive into great detail about every single culture and subculture that has existed throughout the world; that feat can only be accomplished through the work of multiple authors and historians across the world, the experts in their specific field within history itself.

As the writer of this work, I fully recognize that history is inherently biased. Historians choose which stories to tell, and, maybe more importantly, they select which stories to leave out. Oftentimes, historians choose to leave out certain eras or cultures because they simply don't know enough about them. Other times, historians elect to remove certain cultures from the history books because they don't value the contributions of those cultures or civilizations. Personally, I come from a society that is extremely Eurocentric. As much as I try to be objective in my telling of history, I know that my version contains an inherent bias leaning toward this Eurocentric perspective of history simply because of my own cultural and educational background; however, I have made a conscious effort to have this story reflect major cultural movements across the entire globe, with specific inclusion of typically underrepresented cultures and civilizations. By no means did I include all of the important or impactful civilizations and eras across the globe, but I did my best to include civilizations and cultures equitably throughout the book.

We also read about history with our own backgrounds and biases. Each person is influenced by their surroundings, backgrounds, upbringings, and subcultures. Those influences impact the way a person looks at a historical scenario. Will the person bring empathy to a situation where another might see opportunity? Perhaps one's own cultural or ethnic identity will cause that person to empathize with one group over another in a historical story. As readers of history, it is important to acknowledge our own biases and backgrounds; through recognizing ourselves, we can more accurately look at history.

When we study history, we also already have a sense or an awareness about the culture or era we are studying. Whether it's through popular culture or previous schooling, we've likely been exposed to at least a minimal awareness of historical scenarios. You may recognize Ancient Egypt from stories of cursed pyramids and mummies. Maybe you're familiar with the Han Dynasty through the Great Wall of China. Whether you're familiar with his whole story or not, you've probably heard of Christopher Columbus. And you've likely seen photos, watched movies, or played video games that deal with World War I or World War II.

All of this exposure to history shouldn't be ignored either. This background awareness of historical eras brings more context to your further studies of history. As you read about pyramids, imagine that movie you saw with the mummy. When you learn about Han China, think about the photos you've seen of the Great Wall. When you learn about World War II, think about the video game you've played that was set in that era. All of these background experiences will bring more meaning to our studies of history.

Another interesting facet of historical studies comes from the fact that it's not done. History is always changing, which makes learning about it a never-ending process, and it makes writing history a difficult endeavor. Writing a complete history comes from continuing research; our understanding and knowledge about certain eras changes frequently. With new excavations, rediscovered texts, and advanced technology, we are able to rewrite the traditional stories of history at a rapid pace. Interpretations become outdated and new information challenges traditional thinking about cultures, eras, and events. That's part of the reason that I love history. It can be interpreted, misinterpreted, and reinterpreted. That's also what makes the study of history so challenging; there's no right answer. The study of history is as much about storytelling as it is about reinvestigating with an open mind, a clear purpose, and a desire to seek out underrepresented perspectives.

This work moves chronologically as opposed to thematically, even though common themes between distinct cultures will emerge. Much of the information about the cultures and eras that we examine come from both traditional and contemporary historical analysis. Some of these traditional interpretations of history that have been pushed to the forefront of our narrative by primarily European and American historians have been reinterpreted only recently, and many of these reinterpretations have been deemed to be more accurate and well-rounded compared to the traditional interpretations that have emblazoned themselves into our modern lore.

With that said, enjoy your adventure into the story of the world. Read it: explore all the fun, exciting, depressing, and influential eras of history that you can. Wrestle with it: figure out where you stand on certain historical issues and concepts. Criticize it: don't just simply take my words for it. Challenge it: if you find something wrong in this text or in history itself, do something about it. Embrace it: history has already happened and we can't change it, but we can change the way we move forward. But above all, enjoy it: the process of learning about history is fun! History is the story of the world, and it's a true story. Enjoy the story, plot twists, characters, drama, and resolutions that come with this incredible true story.

And the cool thing about this true story is that the ending isn't written yet. We're living somewhere in this story. We are the authors who can continue to write it. We're living in the middle of a chapter, a chapter that we have the power to change, propel, and create ourselves. But for now, it's time to figure how we got to this page.

PART 1

~~~~~

ANCIENT CIVILIZATIONS

CHAPTER 1

ANCIENT SUMER

Mesopotamia - Middle East

4000 B.C.E. to 2000 B.C.E.

~~~~~

The Ancient Sumerians of Mesopotamia created the first civilization in history. The pattern of society that they developed has been copied and expanded upon by nearly every society that followed.

~~~~~

Until about 4000 B.C.E., humans practiced a hunter-gatherer lifestyle. This meant that they woke up each morning and hunted for food, or gathered plants to eat. They used resources that they found on a daily basis to create tools that aided in their hunting and gathering.

This type of lifestyle was not extremely stable. If animal populations migrated, human tribes had to follow the animals in order to continue having something to hunt and eat. If the seasons changed and edible plants went dormant, humans had to migrate to a more favorable location. This meant that the human population of the world lived a nomadic lifestyle, moving from place to place to find food and water.

Along the shores of the Tigris and Euphrates River in Mesopotamia, a revolutionary movement occurred that would completely change the way humans lived for the remainder of history. Humans started farming.

~~~~~

Current historical belief tells us that the Sumerians were the first civilization in the world, which means they were some of the first people to settle in one place, as opposed to hunting and gathering, which was a nomadic lifestyle. The existence of Ancient Sumer was unknown until archaeologists discovered artifacts in modern-day Iraq in the mid-1800s.

The Sumerians existed in an area of the world known as the Fertile Crescent, named for its extremely healthy soil and rivers that make the process of agriculture much easier than other areas of the world. The rivers that flow through Mesopotamia are the Tigris River and the Euphrates River. Mesopotamia actually means "land between two rivers" in Greek. With two fresh water sources, Sumerians had an automatic advantage when it came to establishing the concept of civilization. They flooded regularly, which created fertile soil. This fertile soil allowed the Sumerians to create a food surplus, which gave the society a stable food supply that was primarily grain-based.

The Sumerian food surplus was dependent on their creation of a complex irrigation system, which was a network of canals and dams that channeled water from the rivers into crop fields. Historians believe that the Sumerians invented the plow, which allowed them to become much more efficient farms, especially once they introduced domesticated animals to pull the plow.

Due to its food surplus, Sumerians were able to create a division of labor. One of the byproducts of a division of labor is a social structure. Archaeologists have found evidence of several levels of social classes in Ancient Sumerian society. Kings, priests, government officials, and nobles topped the social ladder. Their houses were likely luxurious: two story mud houses, whitewashed to shine in the sun, and placed in the center of the city.

Merchants, artisans, fishermen, and farmers lived in the middle of Sumer's social pyramid. Evidence of metalwork has been uncovered by archaeologists in Mesopotamia dating back to the Sumerian age. Mesopotamia did not possess any metals of its own so had to trade with neighboring societies to obtain metals for making weapons and tools. Slaves were at the bottom of society in Ancient Sumer. Slaves in the ancient world tended to be enemy captives from war.

At the top of the social pyramid was the king. Kings ruled Sumerian city states with divine right, a belief that the gods favored the king, which gave the king incredible power over the people. The king created and enforced laws, but he also led his army into battle. Frequent wars were fought to defend land, expand land, and over the use of water, the key to success in any civilization. Sumerian armies used both professional soldiers and citizen-soldiers who fought on foot and on chariots.

Kings also appointed government officials to help with the enforcement of laws. The Sumerians created the oldest known system of writing in the world, and they used their writing system to create the first known written record of laws in history. Centuries later, these laws would be the inspiration for Hammurabi's Code, a code created in Mesopotamia by a succeeding civilization in Mesopotamia. Sumerians likely invented writing as a means of accounting. Early Sumerian writing took the form of pictures, which each represented a certain word. Before their writing system evolved to become simpler, their system contained as many as 2,000 symbols; writing was so complex and such a new technology that scribes were enlisted to help. Scribes were people whose sole job was to read and write records. Eventually, literature developed. *The Epic of Gilgamesh* was written during this era; it describes a massive flood that lasted for years and destroyed the whole world, and it probably reflected a real flood that occurred in Mesopotamia, which often happened.

Religious leaders also held a high position in society. Sumer's polytheistic religion was a daily piece of people's lives; average Sumerians tried to please the gods while farming or in settling disputes. Sumerians worshiped their gods in temples, called ziggurats; some of these ziggurats reached as high as seven stories. Historians have interpreted that Sumerians believed their gods lived in the tops of these ziggurats. Religious ceremonies happened frequently, and most included music, while some included ritual human sacrifice.

Aside from major innovations in architecture, the Sumerians created some of the world's most impactful pieces of technological advancement that allowed humans to work more efficiently. They likely invented the wheel; originally, the wheel lay flat so artisans could spin clay pots. Eventually, it was turned on its side and rolled, which became useful for transportation and war.

The Sumerians began to lose power around 2300 B.C.E. when the Akkadians started to gain control over Sumerian city-states. After 300 years, the Akkadians would come to dominate Mesopotamia for the next 250 years before Hammurabi brought the Babylonians to power. Hammurabi would go on to produce what historians consider the first record of law in the world, a format that nearly every civilization would model their own laws after, either directly or indirectly.

Ultimately, though, every civilization that followed the Sumerians used Sumerian methods of success to achieve their own heights. Without Sumerian ingenuity and geographic advantages, would we still be hunter-gatherers? Or was civilization bound to arise somewhere eventually? Regardless, the Ancient Sumerians' process of creating the first civilization completely changed the world.

CHAPTER 2

ANCIENT EGYPT

Egypt - North Africa

3000 B.C.E. to 1000 B.C.E.

~~~~~

Famous for their lasting legacy of pyramids and hieroglyphics, the Ancient Egyptians created one of the most complex and compelling societies in history, one that sparks interest and intrigue into the modern era.

~~~~~

The Ancient Egyptians created one of the first civilizations in the world. Many of their buildings and monuments still stand today, which has made Egypt one of the most intriguing civilizations for historians and adventurers for thousands of years.

Even though Ancient Egypt was settled in the middle of the Sahara Desert, its civilization was structured along the Nile River, which provided the necessary fresh water source for civilization to occur. In fact, a majority of Egypt's population today still lives within a few miles of the Nile River, and the river remains a crucial resources for transportation and irrigation. The Sahara Desert provided a protective barrier to the west, while the Mediterranean Sea provided protection from the north. These barriers allowed Egypt to develop with limited interruption from invading tribes and clans.

The Nile River, the lifeline of Ancient Egypt, provided plenty of fresh water for irrigation. Egyptians were able to grow grain, which gave them a massive food surplus. Once this food surplus was developed, a government was needed to control the flow of goods.

Around the year 2950 B.C.E., King Menes united the upper and lower kingdoms of Egypt, making him the first pharaoh over the entirety of Ancient Egypt. From then on, pharaohs ruled Egypt for nearly 2,000 years. A pharaoh was like a king. When a pharaoh died, the pharaoh's son became the next pharaoh: this system is called a dynasty.

The pharaoh had government officials to help run the government and Egyptian society. An important position was the pharaoh's vizier, his royal advisor. The pharaoh had total control over everything in Egypt; his rule became law.

Egyptians believed that the pharaoh was himself a god - this belief allow the pharaoh to hold onto complete power.

Ancient Egyptians followed a polytheistic religious belief system, which meant they believed in many gods, a common belief in many ancient cultures. A major portion of Ancient Egyptian religious belief centered around the afterlife. When Egyptians died, they would be mummified and buried in a tomb. To be mummified meant that their internal organs were removed and placed in jars. Then, the body was embalmed and wrapped in cloth to preserve it. Ancient Egyptians believed that a person would move into the afterlife with all of the possessions with which they were buried.

Wealthy people were buried in elaborate tombs with all of their worldly riches. When archaeologists uncovered Ancient Egyptian tombs, they were often filled with gold, jewels, and other riches. Ancient Egyptian burial chambers were extremely well-built, and many of them survive to this day. The famous Pyramids of Giza were tombs constructed for pharaohs, as were the ornate statues in the Valley of the Kings. The genius and skill that it took to build these tombs, and the fact that they are still standing after 4,000 years, shows how well Ancient Egyptians used math and architecture to build their civilization.

Historians know so much about Ancient Egypt based on the writing that was preserved on and inside these tombs. Egyptian writing is called hieroglyphics, and they typically look like small pictures. These pictures represented words, and their writing system is one of the oldest, most complete systems in ancient history. For centuries, historians tried to decipher the meaning of Ancient Egyptian hieroglyphics; that all changed with the discovery of the Rosetta Stone in 1799 C.E. The Rosetta Stone was a large stone with a speech inscribed on it in Ancient Egyptian hieroglyphics *and* Greek, a language that historians knew well. They were able to use this to decipher the meaning of hieroglyphics, which unlocked the secrets of the Ancient Egyptian world. Egyptians did not only write on tomb walls; they also wrote on papyrus, a paper-like substance that held up well over time under dry conditions. Ancient Egyptian books, like the *Book of the Dead*, gave historians insight into Egyptian rituals and daily life.

By about 1000 B.C.E., the Ancient Egyptian dynasties began to lose power. Weakened from centuries of battle with the Nubians to the south, the Egyptians would eventually be conquered by the Assyrians, then the Persians, then the Greeks under Alexander the Great, and then the Romans. Egypt's agricultural production became a key resource for any empire in the Mediterranean region, as it could provide enough food surplus for a large population, and that surplus could be exported along the Nile River and distributed throughout the Mediterranean Sea coastline. It would take until the mid-1900s C.E. for Egypt to regain its independence from foreign rulers and see itself governed by an Egyptian again.

Though they remained under foreign control for thousands of years, the foundation that this ancient civilization set formed the basis for the major civilizations that arose in that area for nearly 3,000 years after its capture. Thanks to their incredible legacy left by well-constructed architecture, well-preserved writing, and far-reaching impact, Ancient Egypt has mystified and intrigued historians for centuries.

CHAPTER 3

INDUS RIVER VALLEY

Indus River - India and Pakistan

5500 B.C.E. until about 1800 B.C.E.

~~~~~

Though this civilization set the stage for one of the longest, continuously inhabited places on the map, historians know surprisingly little about the ancient societies of the Indus River Valley.

~~~~~

The Indus River begins high up in the Himalaya, a mountain range that features the world's tallest peaks, like Mt. Everest at 29,000 feet. The snow melt drops rapidly into the high Indian plains and eventually turns into the Indus River.

The Indus River Valley was an ideal region for one of the world's first civilizations. Its wide, flat plains were fertilized by annual floods, and the network of rivers made irrigation relatively easy for farmers to grow enough crops to establish and maintain a food surplus.

Evidence of religious rituals in the Indus River Valley date back as far as 5500 B.C.E. Farming likely began in the valley around 4000 B.C.E., and it took another 1000 years for the people of the valley to develop urban centers along the river. By 2500 B.C.E., dozens of elaborate, well-planned cities existed in the valley.

Archaeological excavations along the Indus River have found evidence of houses with wells for fresh water access, bathrooms, and sophisticated underground drainage systems. Cities featured central bath houses, complete with heated bath tubs that used copper pipes to produce heat. Living conditions for people along the Indus River were better than almost anywhere in the world at the time, including contemporary societies in Babylonian Mesopotamia and Ancient Egypt. In fact, the people of the Indus River Valley likely had contact with Ancient Sumerians and Babylonians. Based on archaeological evidence in the Indus River Valley and writing from Ancient Mesopotamia, historians have determined that the two civilizations traded goods and ideas. Though more research and study is needed to determine the extent of these connections, this shows that ancient civilizations developed interconnected trade routes much earlier than many historians have previously concluded.

Like Ancient Sumer, the Indus River Valley civilization had its own unique writing system. Dozens of records exist; the unfortunate part is that no one has been able to decipher their writing system. Historians have access to so many documents and engraved pieces of Indus River Valley writing, but no one knows what it means (much like no one could decipher Ancient Egyptian hieroglyphics until the discovery of the Rosetta Stone). This is why the Indus River Valley civilization remains one of the least-understood of the world's first civilizations.

Historians know that dozens of advanced cities existed throughout the Indus River Valley, but they don't know what their relationship was. It's unclear whether these cities were independent city-states, or if they were part of a centralized government.

Evidence of distinct religious practice has been found in the ancient city of Balathal, where practitioners believed in the messages of the Vedas, a set of sacred texts that forms the basis of the religion of Hinduism. In the modern world, Hinduism is one of the most practiced religions in the entire world, and its origins date back thousands of years to the Indus River Valley. The major religion in the Indus River Valley was a precursor to Hinduism, but it likely looked much different than the modern religion. Indus River Valley citizens worshipped many gods in a polytheistic religious system. Statues of these gods have been found at multiple sites throughout the Indus River Valley.

Historians do know that the Indus River Valley civilization began to decline. Writing began to disappear, and so did evidence of trade. Entire cities were abandoned. Though historians don't know the reason for the Indus River Valley civilization's decline, the current leading theory suggests that rivers dried up due to drought. This would have interrupted their food surplus, which is the basis for any major civilization. Nomadic herders entered the region from the north and began to occupy the land, marking the end of the great Indus River Valley civilization. It was previously believed that these mountain herders brought the Vedic traditions (and the religion of Hinduism) into India, but recent historical analysis has determined that these mountain herders likely adapted to the religion that was already practiced in the Indus River Valley through cultural diffusion.

The story of the Indus River Valley civilization is currently being written. Unlike Mesopotamia and Ancient Egypt, archaeologists and historians have begun to excavate major sites in the Indus River Valley only recently. Whereas sites in Ancient Egypt have been continually excavated since the late 1700s, excavations in some sites in the Indus River Valley began as late as the 1990s. In fact, sites in the Indus River Valley were of such little interest to early British archaeologists that they used stones from the city of Harappa to construct a railroad, further destroying the chances of developing a complete understanding of the ancient city. As historians and archaeologists continue to learn more about the early civilizations in the area, it is quite possible that they'll determine the Indus River Valley to be the first civilization; recently, historians have theorized that civilization began here much earlier than it did in Mesopotamia.

Though the major civilization of the Indus River Valley had come to a close, this area of Pakistan and India would continue to grow, and it would remain one of the world's most densely populated areas even until the modern day.

CHAPTER 4

ABORIGINAL AUSTRALIA

Australia - Oceania

50,000 B.C.E. to Present

~~~~~

Aboriginal society might be the oldest continuous culture in the world. Its rich history is entirely passed down verbally through generations, forging a bond between ancestors that fights to hold onto tradition in the modern world.

~~~~~

Australia is an island (and a continent) that bridges the Indian and Pacific Oceans south of Indonesia and New Guinea. Its coastal areas produce temperate climates that allow food cultivation, but the interior of the continent contains vast deserts with little vegetation.

Historians and anthropologists believe that humans migrated to Australia from Indonesia and New Guinea between 60,000 and 40,000 years ago. The people who migrated to Australia and made it their home have come to be known as Aborigines.

For thousands of years, Aborigines developed a rich culture in a vibrant landscape. Aborigines developed into hundreds of individual tribes throughout the island, and each tribe had its own unique attributes.

The Aborigines did not develop a written language, but they used cave paintings, verbal storytelling, and song to pass down their history. They also used verbal tradition to pass along their deep understanding of how to survive in the harsh climates of Australia, from the mild coastal territories to the scorching deserts. Each tribe had its own song that they shared at ceremonial events, and sometimes certain dances accompanied these songs.

Music played a major role in Aboriginal culture. With the invention of an instrument called the didgeridoo (a long wooden tube), Aborigines would sing as a way to relay important tribal stories, pass down history, and accompany sacred traditions, like the entrance of a boy in manhood or a girl into womanhood.

Aboriginal religion professed that the world began in the Dreamtime, a time before humans walked the earth, when the ancestors created everything, like the rivers, rocks, and plants. They believed that the ancestors left clues about the

Dreamtime in certain rocks, mountains, and caves; these sites became sacred sites to Aboriginal cultures over the course of tens of thousands of years. Daily religious practices focused on animism, the belief that spirits inhabited everything, including the spirits of those who had gone before them. When an Aboriginal person died, their remains were cremated and, Aborigines believed, the person became a part of the earth. Many tribes painted representations of ancestors on sacred rocks, visiting often to seek guidance and to pay respect.

Though many tribes were hunter-gatherers living a semi-nomadic lifestyle, there is evidence of large-scale agriculture in some parts of Australia that date back thousands of years. There is some evidence that Aborigines even traded and interacted with cultures outside of Australia. Some historians believe that Chinese expeditions from the mid-1400s found Australia and came into contact with Aborigines. Archaeologists have found coins in Australia that date from a 10th century East African kingdom. However, since the Aborigines never wrote their history down, western historians cannot currently corroborate that evidence.

By the time British sailor James Cook came to Australia in 1770 and declared it to be part of the British Empire, it is estimated that there may have been as many as 600 tribes speaking over 250 languages. Unfortunately, the arrival of Europeans meant the arrival of disease, greed, and racism, which decimated Aboriginal populations, and much of their verbal history along with it. In fact, many modern history texts only begin the story of Australian history with the arrival of Europeans, completely ignoring tens of thousands of years of thriving culture. Today, Aboriginal cultures strive to survive after centuries of persecution by British occupation.

PART 2

~~~~~

CLASSICAL CIVILIZATIONS

CHAPTER 5

ANCIENT GREECE

Mediterranean Sea - Europe

800 B.C.E. to 146 B.C.E.

~~~~~

Often viewed by westerners as the pinnacle of ancient culture, the concept of Ancient Greece has been romanticized and glorified for centuries. Its crown jewel, Athens, has shaped western society into the modern era.

~~~~~

Ancient Greece was not an empire in the modern sense of the word. Rather, it was a collection of city-states that each operated independently from one another. Each

Greek city-state was about the size of a modern city, but it acted like its own independent nation, each with its own laws, cultures, and customs.

Since the Greek region was extremely separated by geography, it took a long time for it to unify as a modern nation. The Greek peninsula is very mountainous, and the surrounding sea contains about 2,000 islands. This made it difficult for one city-state to conquer the other. It also made communication difficult, which made it nearly impossible for Ancient Greece to unify under one centralized government.

The city-state of Sparta, for example, was a city-state on the Greek peninsula. It centered around a warrior culture; each male was expected to grow up in military training so that they could serve in the army later on as an adult. Sparta's government consisted of an oligarchy, with two kings and a council of elders that made decisions. Females were expected to learn war techniques as well, though females in Sparta tended to run the government when the men were away at war. In Sparta, things like literature, art, and philosophy were almost looked down upon.

Today, when people reference Ancient Greece, typically they are really talking about Ancient Athens. Athens is championed in history as the founder of democracy and western philosophy. The city of Athens was named for the goddess Athena, the goddess of wisdom in Ancient Greek polytheistic religious beliefs. Sparta looked to Ares, the god of war, as their patron (not surprisingly).

Ancient Athens was not founded with a democratic political system. In fact, it was founded under a tyrannical ruler: a single king. According to legend, around 508 B.C.E., Athenians felt oppressed by their king so they overthrew him in a violent revolution. Once the king was gone, they devised a new governmental system that, as far as historians know, was the first of its kind anywhere in the world.

This new governmental system would come to be known as democracy. In Athenian democracy, all citizens voted for each new law. A group of 500 elected officials would propose a new law to the assembly, which consisted of all Athenian citizens who decided to show up for the vote. There were no political parties, but people would speak out and argue for or against each proposed law to try to persuade other assembly members to vote their way. A vote would pass or fail based on a simple majority vote.

As fair and equal as this system is represented in modern culture, the democracy practiced in Athens was less inclusive than one might imagine, especially considering who the government considered to be a citizen. A citizen was a male over the age of 18 whose father was an Athenian citizen. This meant that females were not considered citizens, thus, they could not vote in the Athenian democracy. Since about one-third of Athens' population were slaves, that meant that only 10 to 20 percent of people who resided in Athens were considered citizens.

This is far from a truly representative government by our modern standards, but one inclusive aspect of Athenian democracy came in the form of social class. It did not matter if you were a rich male or a poor male; you could still vote, and still voice your opinion.

Aside from its democratic experiment, Ancient Athens still shines as the origin of western thought thanks to its golden age. Philosophers like Socrates, Plato, and Aristotle championed new ways of thinking and learning. Architects constructed iconic buildings like the Parthenon. Artists painted lifelike scenes on temple walls, and sculptors created realistic statues of the human body, techniques that would not be seen again until the Italian Renaissance in the 1400s. Writers like Homer scribed stories like *The Iliad* and *The Odyssey*, which still find their way into high school literature classes.

The Ancient Greek city-states even joined together to host the first Olympic games, where they competed in running, jumping, discus throwing, wrestling, boxing, and chariot races. In 330 B.C.E., Athenians built an Olympic Stadium that held 50,000 people, and the stadium still stands today (partly due to some Roman refurbishment).

By 323 B.C.E., a military leader from the city-state of Macedonia called Alexander the Great would conquer all the Greek city-states, and then Egypt, Mesopotamia, and parts of India, which brought brief political unity to the Greek peninsula and surrounding islands. Less than 200 years later, the Greek peninsula would be conquered by an emerging power on the Mediterranean Sea: the Romans. Greeks would not really see independence again until the 1830s C.E., nearly 2,000 years later.

The lasting legacy of Athenian democracy has found its way into the modern world, setting part of the foundation for the United States government, and dozens of other indirect democracies all over the world.

CHAPTER 6

ROMAN REPUBLIC

Italian Peninsula - Europe

509 B.C.E. to 27 B.C.E.

~~~~~

This lesser-known era of the powerful Roman state served as the model for many modern democratic nations. As the small city-state began to expand, it outgrew its attempts at shared leadership, ushering in a new era of Roman dominance.

~~~~~

According to legend, the city of Rome was founded by twins named Romulus and Remus, who were the sons of the war god, Mars, and then abandoned at birth. The myth goes on to tell us that the twins were raised by wolves before rising up to become powerful leaders. When it came time to decide who would rule, the twins fought each other for power. Romulus won the fight; therefore, the city was named Rome. Of course, this is just a myth. Realistically, Rome evolved over centuries, and people slowly developed a functioning society.

Initially, Rome was controlled by a neighboring city-state's king. In 509 B.C.E., around the same time as Athens' democratic revolution, Rome held a revolution of their own. They overthrew the foreign king and installed a government system called a republic, which is an indirect democracy.

Rome's political revolution was not the only innovation necessary to give rise to the powerful city. Rome was built on a swamp; swamps carry diseases and make farming and infrastructure difficult to accomplish. So, Romans architects had to devise a drainage system to keep the stagnant water out of their developing city; this drainage system still exists beneath Rome today.

Through other innovations and strategies, Rome began to create a centralized government, with the city of Rome as its center. The Italian peninsula has a mountain range running through its center, but it is relatively open, which makes conquering and communicating much easier than the Greek landscape. The Romans took over neighboring city-states, eventually controlling major river valleys that could provide a food surplus for the Romans.

As Roman territory began to expand, their society started to develop into a complex social structure. Roman society was separated into two basic social classes: the rich and the poor. The rich were called patricians: they typically came from rich families who owned land, and they held all of the political and economic power in early Rome. The commoners were called plebeians; they consisted of artisans, merchants, and peasants.

Social class played a major role in Roman life, and in government. Their republican form of government evolved over time, but the basic idea remained the same. A republic is a form of indirect democracy, where people vote for someone to represent them in government rather than attending government meetings themselves. Two consuls lead the government; consuls held office for one year. Senators, a group of about 300 wealthy patricians, served in their roles for life once chosen, and their role was to debate and create laws that all citizens had to follow. The assembly rounded out the republic; they were a group of representatives from the plebeian commoner class whose role increased in power as the Republic began to grow in physical size and population.

Each group within the republican government had a specific major function. Roman plebeian citizens, who were adult males, voted for their district's representatives in the assembly. Assembly members voted for the two consuls from the pool of senators. If there was an open senate seat, the consuls would choose which patrician would become the next senator. Each group relied on the other to succeed in voting and in being elected, which created an early form of checks and balances among different levels of government.

The government approved massive building projects that transformed Rome into a modern city. Aqueducts, which are giant open-air water pipes, brought fresh water from the mountains into the cities to provide fresh, running water. The government issued laws and communication in Latin, which became the official language of all Roman territories. Roads were built to connect all parts of the expanding Roman Republic. Roads allowed the centralized government to communicate well, and it allowed the growing Roman military to reach the borders quickly to suppress any revolts that arose.

And revolts arose often. As Rome continued to use military force to invade neighboring territories, the indigenous people fought back. But the organization that Roman soldiers brought to their expansion eventually won almost every time.

Rome brought the same admiration for war into their entertainment and culture. They built giant arenas for chariot races and gladiator games, where slaves would fight each other to the death in front of a cheering crowd. Often, these battles would be dedicated to Mars, the god of war.

With its close proximity to Greece, Romans essentially borrowed Greek polytheistic religion, giving Greek gods Roman names. Zeus, the chief Greek god, became Jupiter in Rome. Ares, the Greek god of war, became Mars in Rome. Massive government buildings were constructed in honor of some of these Roman gods. Dozens of these buildings were constructed in the Roman Forum, which became the center for government operation, political discourse, and the center of downtown Rome, making it one of the only places where patricians and plebeians could interact.

Rome also had a third social class: slaves. Rome contained hundreds of thousands of slaves. When Rome went to war with a neighboring society, they would take war captives and make them slaves. Roman slaves could work for a certain amount of years and potentially become Roman citizens. Slaves built Roman roads, aqueducts, bridges, and buildings. They also fought in gladiatorial games.

By 75 B.C.E., slaves had recognized their power in numbers. Led by a slave named Spartacus, Roman slaves united and revolted against the Roman Republic. Though the slave uprising was eventually squashed by the Roman military, its near-success shocked the order and control of the Roman Republic, especially the patrician class. Senators began to lose power because other government officials lost confidence in their ability to maintain control, while other senators began to collaborate to consolidate power.

Julius Caesar, a Roman general who became a consul, led an army into Gaul (modern-day France and Germany) and won popular support by expanding Roman territory. Through a series of complicated political alliances, Caesar declared himself dictator for ten years. Roman senators recognized Caesar's grab for power, and, feeling threatened by losing their own power, assassinated Julius Caesar on March 15, 44 B.C.E. A senator named Brutus led the assassination, and this is where we get the modern term for "brute".

The assassination of Julius Caesar started a civil war in Rome, which ended in the fall of the republican government system. It did, however, begin a dynastic system that saw Rome ruled by one all-powerful emperor, and it started the era of the Roman Empire that would last for another 500 years.

CHAPTER 7

ROMAN EMPIRE

Mediterranean Sea - Europe

27 B.C.E. to 476 C.E.

~~~~~

The Roman Empire and all its splendor has enchanted the minds of western leaders and commoners alike for two millennia. Rising to leagues of epic grandeur made its fall that much more impactful on the development of the west.

~~~~~

For 500 years, Rome functioned as republic, which was a form of indirect democracy where laws were decided by elected officials, not just a single ruler. All of that changed in 44 B.C.E. with the assassination of Julius Caesar.

Julius Caesar was a general who became consul, and then declared himself dictator for ten years. Senators feared that he was gaining too much power, so they assassinated him at a senate meeting on March 15th, 44 B.C.E. This put Rome into chaos, and the Roman people lost trust in the senate. A civil war broke out that lasted for the next 17 years.

In 27 B.C.E., Julius Caesar's nephew, Octavian, became the Emperor of Rome. He changed his name to Augustus Caesar as a way to reflect the power that his uncle had obtained.

Augustus Caesar's Roman Empire was enormous; it controlled about 57 million people, or about 20 percent of the world's population at the time. It controlled about 1.7 million square miles of territory, ranging from North Africa to the Middle East to Northern Europe, which made it one of the largest empires in history. It controlled Egypt, which provided a majority of its grain supply for its food surplus. Rome's occupation of the entire Mediterranean coastline made trade between different parts of the empire extremely efficient.

As emperor of this huge territory, Augustus went on to approve elaborate and effective government programs that changed the lives of Roman citizens. He commissioned the building of more aqueducts, which channeled water from the mountains into Rome's major urban centers, giving fresh running water to even the poorest people living in downtown Rome. He installed a fire department and police department to keep the people of Rome safe and under control. He built large marble buildings that took the place of Rome's crowded wooden tenements. Of course, he positioned massive marble and bronze statues of himself atop most of these government buildings to assert his power.

In 14 C.E., Augustus Caesar died of old age. For many Roman citizens, Augustus was the only ruler they had ever experienced. Almost immediately, the senate declared that Augustus was a god in the Roman pantheon of gods. Adding gods and goddesses in the Roman polytheistic religion was common.

Augustus' stepson, Tiberius, became the next Emperor of Rome. The use of military force to expand Rome's borders continued under Tiberius and the emperors that followed.

When a new territory was conquered, Rome faced intense hatred from the people they took over, unsurprisingly. Rome counteracted this by allowing the newly conquered territories to keep major pieces of their own culture, as long as they paid their taxes. Newly conquered Romans could even practice their old religions. For example, when Rome conquered the territory of Judea in the Middle East, a majority of the people there practiced the religion of Judaism, and they continued to practice their religion. Most people who lived in newly conquered Roman territories were even allowed to become full citizens of Rome as a way for them to buy into being Roman. They could vote, pay taxes, benefit from Roman building projects, and serve in the military.

Still, Rome faced almost constant threats from its border lands because old tribes and societies wanted their independence back. As Rome's borders continued to expand, it became more difficult to fight off these rebels. Essentially, Rome was always in a state of war.

This attitude and glorification of war found its way into Roman culture through sport, like gladiator battles. Gladiatorial battles grew more popular during the empirical era, and typically featured slaves battling each other to the death in front of a roaring crowd of tens of thousands of people. When the Colosseum was built in 80 C.E., it held 50,000 people. It featured awnings to give the crowd shade. It had underground tunnels and trap doors where gladiators could move and pop out onto the arena. Sometimes, the fights included wild animals, like lions, that would hunt the gladiators as they fought. Later, Colosseum operators would flood the arena in the Colosseum and have small-scale navy battles.

But this entertainment only keep Romans occupied for so long. Eventually, it became obvious that the empire was falling apart. It had grown too big to sustain itself. In 284 C.E., the Roman Empire was split into two pieces: the Western Roman Empire and the Eastern Roman Empire. In 330 C.E., Emperor Constantine even moved the capital city of the Empire from Rome to Constantinople in modern-day Turkey. Constantine also converted to the newer religion of Christianity. The religion of Christianity began in the Roman province of Judea around 30 C.E.; based on the teachings of Jesus, the religion would grow from a branch within the religion of Judaism into a belief system of its own. Once persecuted severely throughout the Roman Empire, Christianity would shortly become the official religion of the empire, creating a lasting effect on the future development of Europe.

Trade began to dwindle in the Western Roman Empire, which included the city of Rome itself. Soldiers were not paid as well as they used to be, and the quality of training and gear suffered. As rebels began to grow stronger, the Roman military grew weaker. At one point, Roman military outposts at the far reaches of the empire went unpaid for months, so they just disbanded and absorbed into the indigenous population.

From the inside, Roman politics had become too corrupt to function properly. So many generals wanted to be emperor that they were willing to assassinate any current emperor. This led to dozens of emperors assassinating each other in a very short timeframe. The Western Roman Empire's government became ineffective and essentially useless.

Eventually, outside forces would push their way through Rome's borders. The Goths invaded downtown Rome in 476, signifying the end of the once-great Roman Empire. The 1,000-year order that Rome brought to Europe had ended, plunging Western Europe into the Dark Ages. The Eastern Roman Empire transitioned into the Byzantine Empire, which saw success for centuries after the west fell to invaders. Latin, the once universal language throughout all of Rome, evolved into regional dialects that would become their own languages, like Spanish, French, and Italian. The great literature, art, and architecture that had made Rome the pinnacle of civilization would disappear from Western Europe for 1,000 years.

CHAPTER 8

HAN CHINA

China - East Asia

206 B.C.E. to 220 C.E.

~~~~~

China has contained an advanced civilization for thousands of years, remaining almost entirely self-sufficient for a majority of that time. With resources, natural barriers, and geographic advantages, the Han Dynasty pushed China into its initial golden age.

~~~~~

Early China developed into a civilization independently, meaning it didn't borrow the concept of civilization from anywhere else; it was an original thought.

China's geographic advantages allowed it to develop a thriving civilization. Two major rivers flow through the center of China: the Yellow River and the Yangtze River. These two rivers flood annually and fertilize the wide plains of eastern China, making farming and irrigation fairly easy. The rivers flow from the highlands in Western China. The Plateau of Tibet, which forms the base of the Himalaya Mountains, served as a natural protective barrier from the west. The Gobi Desert to the north served as protection from nomadic invaders from the Mongolian Steppe. The jungles to the south and the ocean to the east also provided protection.

Since China was so surrounded by natural barriers, it was able to develop into a civilization that was essentially free from outside forces and external influences. China is an extremely resource-rich territory, so it didn't need to seek out other civilizations to trade with because they had everything they needed. As a result, China developed in isolation, meaning it rarely interacted with outside civilizations. Whereas Mesopotamia, Egypt, Greece, and Rome all interacted with each other and borrowed ideas from one another, China developed independently, so its civilization looked much different compared to con-temporary civilizations.

Initially, China was not a unified civilization; it consisted of hundreds of independent city-states that each had their own leaders. For centuries, China was engulfed in an era of turmoil called the Warring States Period. During this time, major city-states fought each other for control of China.

This time period was extremely violent, and it forced leaders to think about the best way to rule China in order to bring about peace. Out of this chaos came the Hundred Schools of Thought, in which philosophers created and presented various leadership methods that a government could use to rule effectively in order to achieve peace. Three major philosophies developed from the Hundred Schools of Thought: Confucianism, Daoism, and Legalism. Confucianism taught that rulers should lead by example, and to treat others as they would want to be treated. Daoism taught that rulers should govern as little as possible, and that people gain peace and happiness by living simply and in harmony with nature. Legalism taught that leaders should rule strictly, and that more laws with harsh punishments would translate into more peace. Emperors throughout China's long imperial history would employ various styles of these three leadership methods.

At the end of the Warring States era, one city-state's leader, Qin Shi Huang, conquered all of China through war, which created a centralized government. This unified China for the first time under a single ruler, or emperor, ushering in the Qin Dynasty, which lasted from 221 to 206 B.C.E. In fact, Emperor Qin (pronounced chin) is where the name "China" originated.

The early Chinese emperor professed that he had the right to rule through the Mandate of Heaven. The Mandate of Heaven declared that the emperor was given the right to rule from divine power.

Emperor Qin utilized the governing philosophy of Legalism, and imposed harsh punishments for anyone who got in the way of his authority. As he grew older, he became obsessed with the concept of immortality, or living forever. He was led to believe that drinking mercury would give him immortality; in reality, mercury is extremely poisonous, and, ironically, it led to the emperor's early death. Emperor Qin was buried in a massive tomb that was surrounded by over 8,000 unique terracotta warriors. Legend suggests that the tomb has a river of mercury running through it as well. Though only a small percentage of the tomb has been excavated by archaeologists, historians have estimated that Emperor Qin's tomb is the largest burial complex in the history of the world.

With the death of Emperor Qin, a new emperor from another family took power, ushering in the beginning of the Han Dynasty that would last for the next 400 years. The Han Dynasty period was a golden age for China, meaning it was a time of peace, economic prosperity, and cultural innovation. The Han emperors relaxed the harsh ruling style of legalism and adopted a more Confucian approach to government.

During this era, the Chinese invented modern paper, allowing Chinese government officials to keep records and easily pass information throughout their massive centralized government.

The Han established a bureaucracy, which meant that the most qualified person would perform a job in government, not just the wealthiest or those who were born into an elevated social class. Citizens of Han China would take civil service exams, which allowed the government to determine who was most qualified for a certain job or role. This created social mobility for all citizens, allowing those born in a lower social class to advance, while allowing those born into a higher social class to fall if they did not produce enough skill.

Typically, in a social structure, peasants, or farmers, were not well-respected, but that was not the case during the Han Dynasty. Those who farmed and grew crops were seen as respected in society due to the Daoist idea that one receives peace by working closely with nature.

Chinese agriculture focused on the staple crop of rice, which grew well in China's low-elevation plains. Chinese farmers invented the wheelbarrow to transport materials more easily, along with the chain pump, which allowed them to move water to higher elevation.

Salt was a major economic material that was plentiful in China. Salt in the ancient world was worth its weight in gold because it allowed people to preserve meat and vegetables before the invention of the freezer. While digging for salt, early Chinese peasants indirectly discovered natural gas, so during the era of the Han Dynasty, peasants heated their homes and lit their stoves with natural gas that funneled through bamboo pipes.

Another major economic product created in China was a fabric called silk: a comfortable, luxurious fabric that could only be produced in China. The silkworm, which only existed in China, produces long strands of silk, almost like a spiderweb. During the Han Dynasty, textile workers invented a machine that wove silk strands together into a fabric, which made it easy to access for people who lived in China's cities. Over time, silk would be in high demand in faraway places, like Rome, which would spark an interest in trade routes between Europe and Asia, bringing other civilizations into contact with the self-sufficient, well-orchestrated civilization of China.

Though the Han Dynasty would end in 220 C.E., other emperors from other families would take their place, implementing their own governing philosophies. Though ruling families changed, China's government system and civilization would remain relatively unchanged until the 1900s, making it one of the most continuous civilizations in history.

PART 3

~~~~~

TRADE AND CULTURAL DIFFUSION

CHAPTER 9

SILK ROAD

Europe and Asia

130 B.C.E. to 1453 C.E.

~~~~~

The Silk Road united civilizations and cultures that previously were unaware of each other's existence. Through this series of interconnected trade routes, the Silk Road spread goods and ideas, and changed the landscape of human geography.

~~~~~

Contrary to what its name suggests, the Silk Road was not a neatly paved road made of silk. The Silk Road was a series of trade routes that connected the eastern world with the western world.

Before 130 B.C.E., China was a self-sufficient, isolated empire that was extremely resource rich. Silkworms existed exclusive in China, and Chinese weavers invented machines that could weave silk into a fabric that was luxurious, comfortable, and colorful.

Meanwhile, the Roman Republic was nearing its peak along the Mediterranean Sea. Wealthy Romans were looking for anything to elevate their social status, especially clothing that gave the appearance of luxury and exclusivity.

In 130 B.C.E., the Chinese emperor of the Han Dynasty opened its borders to trade with the outside world. Chinese merchants could now purchase silk, which was only available in China, and bring it to a town hundreds of miles west, and sell it for a higher price to make a profit. The person who purchased it from the Chinese trader could travel hundreds more miles west and sell it in another town for an even higher price. Eventually, that same piece of silk that began in China could end up about 5,000 miles away in downtown Rome.

That piece of silk would be traded between dozens of merchants before reaching Rome, and each time the cost to purchase it would rise. So, by the time it reached Rome, it would be exponentially more expensive that its original cost in China.

In Rome, the supply of silk was low; Romans didn't have access to it unless multiple merchants made extremely long journeys. Because silk was such a rare item, the demand for it was high; all the rich people wanted it.

Silk was not the only item traded along the Silk Road; it was just the most famous and fetched the highest price. Items like salt, precious metals, spices, and gems were popular trading goods along the Silk Road, too. These items were light to carry and they could be sold for a high price at distant markets due to the high demand for these rare goods.

Though merchants profited tremendously from trading items along the Silk Road, the journey was oftentimes extremely dangerous. Travelers had to move through China's natural barriers, like the Gobi Desert or the base of the Tibetan Plateau, where they would brave extreme heat and cold. Traders had to travel with pack animals like camels, which required water and food, so they needed to have a guaranteed water source, or pack enough supplies to survive long parts of the journey. The fact that the Silk Road was so profitable was a danger all its own. Thieves and bandits hid along mountain passes and frequently stole goods from traders. The dangers from physical features, climate, and bandits caused prices for goods to rise even more.

Material goods weren't the only things traded along the Silk Road; ideas were exchanged as well. Through a process called cultural diffusion, traders and merchants from multiple cultures would exchange ideas, technology, and beliefs with each other. If a trader came from China to Samarkand, that trader could come in contact with traders from the Mediterranean region. When they weren't trading, they were eating meals together, sharing space together in marketplaces, and talking with each other about subjects that did not involve silk. They would discuss politics and government, which looked different in their respective regions. They discussed and shared new technologies with each other. Through these discussions and experiences with other cultures, ideas were transferred from one society to the next.

During these casual discussions and conversations, traders and merchants would also discuss religion and cultural practices with each other. This is partly how religions like Buddhism and Islam spread outward from their original founding cultures. Buddhism, which began in India around the 5th century B.C.E. based on the teachings of the Buddha, would eventually spread to China over the course of centuries via trade routes along the Silk Road, becoming one of the most practiced religions in the world. Islam, which began on the Arabian Peninsula based on the teachings of Prophet Muhammad, would become the second-largest religion in the modern era. The sharing of religion brought more respect, understanding, and tolerance to the regions along the Silk Road; few religious restrictions were imposed in order to further trade, as opposed to places in Europe that rarely interacted with different cultures than their own.

Though the Silk Road's most famous routes moved over land from China to the Mediterranean, there were also sea routes that moved from China to India, and to the Middle East near Egypt. This brought even more cultures in contact with each other and furthered cultural diffusion along these trade routes as they became more and more intertwined. Port cities along these shipping routes became major centers of culture and commerce. Some of these port cities created their own connecting overland routes to reconnect to the Silk Road.

Historians say that the Silk Road lasted from 130 B.C.E. until 1453 C.E., but that range of dates is a bit misleading. The Silk Road saw highs and lows in popularity over the course of 1600 years depending on the political situation in certain regions along the trade routes. Depending on the emperor's governing philosophy, China sometimes closed its doors to trade, which limited access to silk. Wars and skirmishes in the Middle Eastern highlands caused certain key mountain passes to become unavailable at times. During the Crusades, a major series of wars between European Christians and Middle Eastern Muslims, trade routes that passed through the crucial city of Jerusalem were dangerous and often inactive. In the 13th century, when the Mongol Empire took over a majority of the territory that composed the Silk Road, trade flourished and expanded to levels it had not seen before.

Eventually, by 1453, the new Chinese emperor decided to stop trade with other cultures and restored a policy of strict isolation. This definitively ended the prosperity of the Silk Road because the key products that flowed from China stopped flowing. Then, in 1492, overland routes from Europe to China became obsolete as trade between Europe and the New World of North and South America became the primary focus.

The legacy of the Silk Road is one of trade and economic prosperity as much as it is a legacy of cultural diffusion and the spread of ideas. Without the Silk Road, the cultural shape of Europe, Asia, and the Middle East would look entirely different and our understanding of world cultures would look entirely new.

CHAPTER 10

MALI EMPIRE

Mali - West Africa

1230 C.E. to 1400s C.E.

~~~~~

Ruled by the wealthiest person in human history, the empire of Mali used its advantageous position along the Niger River to create a trade network that flourished in the Middle Ages.

~~~~~

The empire of Mali was a result of the prosperous and advanced empires that came before it. The city-state of Ghana began to gain power in the 6th century through trade. The Niger River acted as a superhighway between the north and south, and the east and west, due to its path.

By the 7th century, Ghana had gained so much wealth and influence through trade that other city-states absorbed themselves into Ghana's sphere of influence. Ghana's influence in the area lasted until the 13th century before it began to lose power and control over its neighboring territories. During this brief period of turmoil, the city-state of Mali took power through trade, alliances, and military force.

In 1230, Sundiata, the Lion King, took full control of the surrounding territories and founded the empire of Mali. The Mali Empire stretched from the Atlantic Ocean to the border of the Sahara Desert to the border of the Africa's dense interior jungles.

In its northern desert territories, Mali possessed a wealth of salt deposits. Salt was extremely valuable in the hot, humid African continent because it allowed for a food surplus to be stored for long periods of time, and it allowed the human body to absorb more water. Due to its necessity in the region (and the world at that time) it fetched a high price in trade.

Southern Mali contained a wealth of gold deposits throughout its territory, which fetched a high price everywhere in the world. In fact, salt in the ancient world was worth its weight in gold.

This exchange of gold and salt meant that Mali possessed two of the most in-demand goods of the ancient world, and they possessed a lot of both. This brought the empire insane amounts of wealth.

In 1312, Mansa Musa became king of the Mali Empire. As emperor, he became the sole owner of all the gold and salt within his domain; because of this, historians and economists have deemed Mansa Musa the richest person of all time. Historians and economists estimate that Mansa Musa was worth about 400 billion dollars by comparison to modern-day definitions of wealth.

As a devout Muslim, Mansa Musa took his pilgrimage to Mecca in 1324. Along this pilgrimage, Mansa Musa traveled through cities like Cairo and exchanged information and culture along the way. This journey was beyond extravagant. It's estimated that Mansa Musa took 12,000 slaves and servants along the journey, and each slave carried four pounds of gold. He took hundreds of camels that each carried pounds of gold. When the caravan passed through cities and towns, Mansa Musa and his servants would throw gold to the people that lined the streets to see the parade. According to some sources, during Mansa Musa's journey through Egypt, he filled an entire room in the Sultan's palace with gold. The price and value of gold dropped exponentially around the entire Mediterranean Sea due to Mansa Musa's extravagance; the supply of gold went up, so the demand went down. This affected the entire Mediterranean economy.

The legend of Mansa Musa's untold wealth reached Europe, and Spanish mapmakers even included Mansa Musa's image on their maps, in which he typically held a beaming piece of gold.

Mansa Musa built up the city of Timbuktu as the heart of the Mali Empire. Its position along the northern part of the Niger River meant that traders from the south could access it easily via boat, and it was the first stop for salt caravans moving south from the Sahara Desert. Timbuktu became a center of trade and cultural diffusion, where people from multiple parts of the Muslim world could come together and bond over a common religion while comparing different ideas from different regions of Africa.

As a result, Timbuktu became one of the most intellectual and sophisticated cities in the world in the 1300s. Timbuktu's libraries were full of new ideas from across Africa and the Middle East, like algebra and astronomy. Its mosques, Islamic places of worship, were some of the most sought-after cultural centers in the world. They provided education to both men, women, and children who learned to read and do math in a more advanced way than anyone in Europe would see for another 100 years.

Mansa Musa ruled over the Mali Empire for about 25 years. When he died, his sons took power through the dynastic system, but they lacked the vision and leadership skills to advance the empire, much less maintain it. Some historians also believe that Mansa Musa squandered much of his empire's wealth during his pilgrimage, which put unnecessary economic strain on Mali. The Mali Empire fell into disarray and shrank over the course of the next century, leaving room for another West African state to take its place.

The 1400s would see the rise of the Songhai Empire, which would occupy and control much of what used to belong to Mansa Musa's Mali Empire, but it would not quite reach the same level of wealth, prosperity, and cultural advancement that the Mali Empire brought to the world.

CHAPTER 11

GREAT ZIMBABWE

Zimbabwe - Southeast Africa

1000 C.E. to 1450 C.E.

~~~~~

Though Great Zimbabwe was a small city-state by land size, its impact was far-reaching. Using trade as a catalyst, Great Zimbabwe merchants were in regular contact with far-flung cultures, which brought cultural diffusion to their own doorstep.

~~~~~

Nestled at the southern end of the Great Rift Valley, the Zimbabwe territory featured multiple rivers that flowed through flat, open woodland. It was an ideal place for a civilization to arise, and it did under the Shona people.

The city-state of Great Zimbabwe rose to power around the year 1000 based on its food surplus of cattle and grain. But it had another, less edible resource that propelled its rise: gold.

With its proximity to the Indian Ocean, traders from Great Zimbabwe were able to connect to the already-bustling sea trade routes that flowed between East Africa, the Middle East, and India. Traders from Great Zimbabwe traded gold for spices and pottery across the Indian Ocean. In fact, ruins of Chinese pottery have been found in the ruins of Great Zimbabwe.

Since Shona traders were in contact with merchants from China, India, and the Middle East, it meant that they were part of a network of intellectual cultural diffusion that existed along this trade network. This cultural diffusion and trading success brought the city-state of Great Zimbabwe enormous wealth.

The city of Great Zimbabwe itself contained ornate and complex buildings that swirled inward with ornate rock design. A building known as the Great Enclosure was likely a royal palace and a grain storage facility; its walls spiraled inwards to protect the royal family and the precious grain. The walls of this facility were expertly designed, sloping downwards to prevent flooding and to enhance wall stability.

Aside from royal palaces, the city contained hundreds of houses and buildings for common people in a vibrant urban center. Most people lived in the wide valley below the Great

Enclosure and tower fort; in the valley, they could farm while under the protection and watchful eye of their rulers.

Historians believe that Great Zimbabwe operated under strict guidelines for gender roles. Males were the head of the household and competed with neighboring males for status in society. Women were expected to farm. Unmarried men were often given to a household as a dependent; if a household had multiple dependents, they received higher societal status. The number of cattle that a household possessed also raised or lowered a house's status.

At its peak, the city-state of Great Zimbabwe housed about 20,000 people, but that was just one city-state among more than 300 similar cities in the larger Shona territory. Archaeologists have found newer houses constructed on the outskirts of the valley floor, which indicates that the city grew rapidly outward.

By the early 1400s, the city-state's success had become its own downfall. The city became overpopulated; to compensate for the large population, the farmland around Great Zimbabwe's bustling city had been overused in attempts to produce enough food for its people. Mass deforestation and overused land led to a food shortage. The city's gold deposits ran low, and trade between Great Zimbabwe and East Africa's coastline slowed to a stop. Eventually, the great stone city was abandoned as people moved to more sustainable areas in the thriving Shona territory.

When Portuguese traders arrived in the 1530s, they referred to the buildings as ruins, meaning the flourishing civilization of Great Zimbabwe had already vanished. Perpetuating racist ideologies, Portuguese traders, who didn't believe that Africans could build such extravagant cities, surmised legends as to who could have built them. European invaders thought that they could have been the legendary mines of King Solomon, or the city of the Queen of Sheba.

The ruins exist to this day; actually, the name of the modern country of Zimbabwe comes from the ruins themselves. Zimbabwe is Bantu for "stones houses", referring to the ruins of this once-great trading empire that existed in southeast Africa.

PART 4

~~~~~

CIVILIZATIONS COLLIDE

CHAPTER 12

MEDIEVAL EUROPE

Western Europe
476 C.E. to 1450 C.E.

~~~~~

After the fall of the Roman Empire, Europe took a nosedive in every sense of the phrase. From culture to intellectual advancement, Europe would struggle to regain relevance in world history for 1,000 years.

~~~~~

By the early 300s, the Roman emperor, who controlled essentially all of Europe, determined that the empire was too large for one emperor to control, so he split the empire into two halves. The Eastern Roman Empire, later known as the Byzantine Empire, had far more economic power and military strength; the Western Roman Empire began to lose power quickly.

After political instability from within, and after multiple invasions from outside civilizations ready to take back the land that Rome had occupied for so long, Rome fell to invading Germanic tribes in 476. The continent of Europe, which had been extremely organized under the Roman Empire, was now driven into a state of chaos.

Without a stable government and economy, people needed to spend their time finding and making food and shelter. There was no time for old Roman luxuries like reading, math, epic buildings, inventions, etc. Within a few generations, everyone in Rome fell into the Dark Ages, a time when knowledge was lost, food was scarce, and survival was difficult.

In this chaos, tribal leaders would gain power by acquiring a larger military force than neighboring clans. Farmland was contested violently and regularly, so tribal leaders built defensive fortresses to defend their land. Over the course of a few hundred years, through alliances, wars, and marriages, these small land-owning tribes became small kingdoms that controlled Europe throughout the medieval era.

Throughout the Roman Empire, everyone spoke the language of Latin. After Rome fell, individual kingdoms that were separated by major physical features would still speak Latin, but it would morph into individual dialects, which eventually became their own languages. This is where we derive the modern languages of Spanish, French, Italian, Romanian, and Portuguese.

The Roman Empire left another stamp on the medieval society that came after it: religion. In 380, Christianity became the official religion of the Roman Empire. Once Europe plunged into the Dark Ages, the religion of Christianity became the central force in Europe. Every town had a church or cathedral in its center. The area around the church served as the main marketplace, and people gathered there for major festivals or holidays, which were based on the church's calendar. In a time of such chaos and instability, the church served as a center for organization and stability for the people of Europe. They collected money to give to people who were poor or sick, they provided education to those who could afford it, and they established monasteries where volunteers could dedicate their lives to the work of the church. Monks in monasteries were often the only people who could read or write in Europe during the Middle Ages.

By about the year 1000, the Catholic Church became the largest landowner in Europe, and during the medieval era, land equaled wealth. This wealth increased the power and influence of the church. The church used some of this wealth to build massive cathedrals and churches throughout Europe, many of which still stand today. These building were the pinnacle of architectural technology in the European Middle Ages; some cathedrals stood as high as 30 stories.

The Roman Catholic Church also held the power of giving kings their blessing, which gave individual kings more power. In such a religious society, a blessing from the church meant that all civilians recognized the legitimacy of that king who received the blessing.

Aside from the church, kings received power by their ability to protect. Throughout the early medieval era, a sea-faring people from the north called Norsemen, or Vikings, led a series of raids on mainland Europe, which created a need for protection. The feudal system developed as a result of these raids.

In the feudal system, kings owned large territories of land, which they granted to lords and nobles, who would rent their land to peasants, or serfs, who farmed the land. These serfs needed to pay taxes to the lords, and the lords paid taxes to the king. Lords paid knights to defend their territories from other invading armies, with the stipulation that all knights would fight for the king in a time of war. Eventually, the population of knights grew too numerous; knights would invade neighboring territories frequently, making Europe extremely dangerous.

The Pope, the leader of the Roman Catholic Church, saw an opportunity to shift that violence to benefit Europe. The Pope declared a Crusade, or holy war, on the Muslim-controlled city of Jerusalem, where the religion of Christianity began. Tens of thousands of European soldiers volunteered to go fight in Jerusalem. The Pope declared it to be a religious war against Muslims, even though both Christians and Muslims worship the same God. This helped to clear Europe of overpopulation, and it also gave kings and nobles an opportunity to increase their social status with a victory. Kings who took more land during the battle would increase their wealth, and they would control the trading center of the Silk Road in this key section of the Middle East.

After nine Crusades, the Muslim empires eventually maintained control of Jerusalem. During these wars, Europeans came in contact with the intellectual thought, technologies, and philosophies of the Muslim-controlled Middle East, which was going through a golden age. These ideas were brought back to Europe through cultural diffusion, and eventually sparked the Renaissance, or rebirth, of Europe in the early 1400s. After nearly 1,000 years, Europe finally emerged from the Dark Ages.

CHAPTER 13

MIDDLE EASTERN CALIPHATES

Middle East and North Africa

622 C.E. to 1453 C.E.

~~~~~

As the religion of Islam gained influence in the Middle East, so did the drive to innovate. Through a confluence of cultural development, Islamic Caliphates produced some of the world's most innovative ideas that continue to impact the modern era.

~~~~~

When the Prophet Muhammad founded the religion of Islam in the early 7th century, he and his followers controlled a key trading center in the Middle East: the city of Mecca. After Muhammad's death, various leaders took over divisions of the religion of Islam. These leaders were known as caliphs: political rulers who also claimed religious authority. Caliphs served a dual role of emperor and high priest.

Through trade and military takeover, Islamic empires controlled Spain, North Africa, and the Middle East by 750. The city of Baghdad in modern Iraq became the capital city of one of these caliphates, the Abbasid Empire.

Baghdad was located at a center point between North Africa, Europe, and Asia. It was a trading center along the Silk Road, and a place where multiple cultures and ideas were exchanged on a regular basis through trade. Its geographic location helped spark a golden age in the city of Baghdad. Some historians refer to this era as the Golden Age of Islam.

During this golden age, Islamic empires demonstrated advances in tolerance, acceptance, and inclusion of different races and ethnicities. Though the most common and official state religion was Islam, Christians and Jews were accepted into society as well. Muhammad taught that Jews and Christians were "people of the book" with a common tradition and general belief system, as all three religions worshipped the same god. Christians and Jews were accepted into caliphate society as full citizens, though some had to pay higher taxes depending on the ruling caliph's policies or the specific territory in which they settled. Overall, this would prove to be one of the most religiously tolerant civilizations in history.

Throughout the Islamic territories, the language of Arabic was spoken by most people. As a result, new ideas could be easily transferred from one part of the empire to the next because there was no need to translate. Books could be published in Baghdad and a scholar in Timbuktu or Cordoba could read it and learn from these new intellectual thoughts.

Major advances were made in the area of architecture, or building. The city of Baghdad, for example, used 100,000 workers who took four years to build the new capital city. It featured palaces, mosques, schools, orphanages, and hospitals; it was aesthetically designed as a perfectly round city.

In 830, architects constructed a large, open a building called the House of Wisdom in the center of Baghdad. Here, some of the world's greatest scholars worked to advance intellectual thought based on the Islamic focus of scholarship. They uncovered ancient Greek, Roman, and Indian texts from thinkers like Plato and Aristotle and translated their works into Arabic so everyone in their empire could access these ideas. Major advances were made in zoology: the study of animals. In the field of astronomy, Muslim scholars were the first to accurately chart the Earth's rotation, as well as accurate moon cycles, and they based the Islamic calendar on these moon cycles.

Scholars in the House of Wisdom also focused on more practical advancements. Inventors created advances in waterworks, building dams and aqueducts to provide water for households, mills, and fields, even incorporating water wheels for irrigation and machine movement.

Muslim scholars placed a heavy focus on geography. They divided the world into climate zones that remain accurate in the modern era. Knowing that the Earth was round hundreds of years before Europeans, Muslim scholars accurately calculated the Earth's circumference, which allowed them to create some of the world's most accurate maps of the era. A scholar in Muslim Spain even produced a world atlas with dozens of maps that featured lands in Europe, Africa, and Asia. Though these maps might look inaccurate by today's standards, they were the most accurate maps produced during that era. Through cultural diffusion, Muslim inventors were able to take the Chinese invention of the compass and adapt it to create a much more portable device that increased its spread and use.

While researching ancient works of Babylon, India, and Greece in the House of Wisdom, a scholar named Al-Khwarizmi created algebra, which in Arabic translates to "the reunion of broken parts". These scholars crafted their mathematical innovations in Arabic numerals, which are the numerals we use today in mathematics. Through this innovation, they popularized the Indian concept of zero, which is Arabic for "something empty". Without the concept of zero, advanced mathematics would be nearly impossible.

Advances in medical science shaped the way we approach medicine in the modern era. Islamic empires had hospitals that were open to all people. These hospitals had separate sections for people with spreadable diseases. Scholars even discovered that infections were caused by bacteria. These advances were charted in Ibn Sina's *Canon of Medicine*, which remains a prominent medical book in the modern era. Muslims in the Abbasid Empire understood the concept of diet, exercise, and antibacterials as a way to live longer.

Even before the various caliphates controlled the Middle East, Arabs had a rich history of storytelling and poetry; this tradition lasted and even increased throughout the Golden Age of Islam. On Papersellers' Street in Baghdad, there were over 100 bookstores. Popular story collections like *A Thousand and One Nights* have lasted until the modern day, with the popular story of *Aladdin* making it into popular American culture.

Ornate calligraphy turned words into their own art form. Music became a major art form as well, with Muslims establishing music schools in Cordoba, Spain, the first music schools in Europe. Recreational activities like polo and chess were created during this era and became popular pastimes.

The Golden Age of Islam would decline as strict Ottoman Turks began to overtake the territory, discouraging scholarship and intellectual advancement. As European Christians invaded Muslim-controlled lands during the Crusades, information and advancements from the Golden Age of Islam would spread through cultural diffusion to European kingdoms, sparking the Renaissance and the end of the European Dark Ages. Former Islamic territories in

Spain and Portugal would use the advancements in geography, transportation, and mathematics to chart new courses across far-flung oceans, sparking the Age of European Discovery that would change the course of history.

CHAPTER 14

MONGOL EMPIRE

Mongolia - Asia

1206 C.E. to 1368 C.E.

~~~~~

Infamous in the west as a raging barbarian, Genghis Khan developed the largest contiguous empire of all time, instituting levels of culture and civilization that would not be seen again until the modern era.

~~~~~

The Mongolian Steppe is located north of China. Its high-elevation grassland that contains little resources, possesses a cold, dry climate, and features wide-open spaces with little natural resources. Traditional Mongolian lifestyle was extremely rugged as a result of their climate and landscape. Without a major freshwater source, farming was difficult. This created a society in which small bands of nomadic people would move from place to place in search of resources, using military force to steal resources from other groups, or occasionally trading for resources that they needed when they possessed something of value. For centuries, the people of the Mongolian Steppe lived in small, segmented tribes that often feuded with each other, rather than existing as a unified, organized civilization.

This was the environment that Genghis Khan was born into in 1162. Originally, his name was Temujin, but he would later become famous under the name "Genghis Khan", which almost literally translates to "universal ruler".

As a child, Genghis Khan's clan abandoned him and his family after the death of his father, who was the clan's leader. Genghis Khan had to survive the rugged winters and landscapes of the Mongolian Steppe to keep his family alive, often going days without food.

On the wide-open plains of the Mongolian Steppe, transportation by horseback was almost a necessity. Most Mongol children were taught to ride horses before they could walk, and they continued their training as they grew. Genghis Khan was no different; he used his skill on horseback and with a bow to hunt game for his family during their isolation.

When Genghis Khan was a teenager, his step-brother hunted a bird and kept it for himself; Genghis Khan found out about this decision and killed his step-brother with an arrow. The environment on the Mongolian Steppe was ruthless.

At age 16, Genghis Khan would marry a young woman named Borte from another tribe. As a wedding gift, Borte's father gave Genghis Khan a black fur coat, a prized possession in frozen Mongolia. Genghis Khan gave this gift to the chief of another tribe in order to forge an alliance. Through this alliance, Genghis Khan eventually gained control over one tribe's military, and he conquered all of the surrounding tribes, eventually uniting the Mongols under his reign as Genghis Khan.

After uniting the Mongols through war and treaties, Genghis Khan went on to invade his neighbors to the south: China. China was the pinnacle of civilization in East Asia; their cities were filled with food, riches, and resources. Every soldier in Genghis Khan's well-trained, tough army of Mongols fought on horseback, which was unheard of in ancient warfare, and it gave the Mongols an incredible advantage in every battle.

With China now under Mongol control, the Mongols brought some of China's most advanced thinkers to the capital of Mongolia in order to learn from them. These scholars brought knowledge of written language, advanced medicine, government structures, and military technology, like gunpowder. The Mongols were masterful at incorporating new ideas into their own culture from the societies that they conquered.

After conquering and controlling nearly the entirety of East Asia, the Mongols would move west to take over modern-day Uzbekistan, Kazakhstan, Russia, and Persia. They even pushed into Europe, the Middle East, and Egypt. After taking control of nearly all of Asia, pieces of Europe, and pieces of Africa, the Mongols would control the largest contiguous empire in history (making them the second-largest empire of all-time next to the British Empire of the 18th century).

Under Mongol rule, Eurasia would experience a peaceful century that historians refer to as the *Pax Mongolica*. Mongol government restored the Silk Road and made trade easier, more efficient, and more prosperous because they controlled all of it. They embraced diversity within their empire. Citizens of the Mongol empire were allowed to practice any religion they wanted, as long as they paid their taxes. And, not only was religious diversity tolerated, but it was encouraged. Genghis Khan hosted Muslim, Christian, Buddhist, Daoist, and Mongol religious thinkers in his court so that he could hear from all represented religions in his empire.

All ethnicities and races were accepted as equals, though realistically the original Mongols were seen as elevated above all other ethnicities. The ideas and customs of all cultures under Mongol control were absorbed as valid, and Mongol government officials aimed to learn about and incorporate new customs into Mongol society.

Genghis Khan instituted systems into his government policy that far outpaced any ruler in the world at that time. The Mongols established a system of public education that wouldn't be seen again in the world until the mid 1800s.

They installed a system of message delivery that allowed a lone horseman to deliver a message to one outpost, where another horseman would take it to the next outpost; this system looked a lot like the Pony Express and made message delivery extremely efficient.

The Mongol military force was unstoppable, and they continued to expand, until the death of Genghis Khan on August 18th, 1227. After his death, his sons and grandsons would split the empire into multiple states. Many of these leaders would exhibit poor leadership skills, and the Mongol Empire disintegrated quickly. Although the Mongol Empire officially ended as quickly as it began, it left a lasting impression on Asia.

Kublai Khan, Genghis Khan's grandson, would end up ruling China, creating the Yuan Dynasty that would rule until 1368. Keeping with his grandfather's tradition of learning from all cultures, he hosted the legendary Marco Polo (a European Christian) in his court, whose book popularized the legacy of Kublai Khan in the west. The Mughal Empire, who ruled India until 1857, claimed to descend from Mongol lineage.

The legacy of the Mongols continues to fascinate historians and archaeologists. After Genghis Khan's death, an anonymous author wrote *The Secret History of the Mongols*, a story about Genghis Khan's life for the royal family. This book became extremely rare until its translation from old Mongolian into modern Mongolian by a modern Mongolian scholar in the early 1900s. Once translated into a modern language, the book forced historians to rethink their interpretations of Genghis Khan and the Mongol Empire. According to *The Secret History of the Mongols*, Genghis Khan, the famous leader of the Mongol Empire, was buried in a mysterious location somewhere on the Mongolian Steppe, a location that has yet to be discovered.

CHAPTER 15

FEUDAL JAPAN

Japan - Asia

1100s C.E. to 1868 C.E.

~~~~~

This era of Japanese history was ripe with conflict and tension. It also gave rise to the legendary samurai who battled nobly to protect their land during this divisive period.

~~~~~

Japan is an island chain off the northern coast of Asia. It has a long history of habitation and it is steeped in rich cultural traditions. Japan is a mountainous archipelago with little flat land for agriculture, but it used innovation to maximize its food production by harvesting rice as its main staple crop because rice doesn't require a lot of land space to grow.

The fact that Japan is an island chain made its resources even more limited, forcing the Japanese to trade with neighboring kingdoms across the seas, like China and Korea. This produced cultural diffusion, bringing concepts like written language and Buddhism to Japan.

The family unit was the main focus in Japanese society. Each family made enough food to sustain themselves, and maybe enough to trade for other goods. The father was the head of the family, and it was the family's responsibility to protect their own land.

Japan was ruled by an emperor through a dynastic system, where descendants of the emperor would rise to power when the emperor died. By 1180, the emperor's power was weak. This allowed powerful families that owned a lot of land to take control of politics in Japanese society. These landowning families used their riches and influence to hire private armies of soldier called samurai, who were hereditary warriors that were loyal and self-disciplined.

Each wealthy landowner also leased land to peasants, who would work the land. Unlike most societies in the world, peasants in Japan were not at the bottom of the social pyramid because working with nature was an important social priority. This priority was largely influenced by the native Japanese religion of Shintoism, and acted in accordance with the Buddhist ideal of simple living. Merchants were at the bottom of the social pyramid because they did not actually make anything; they just traded. In actuality, though, merchants because very wealthy.

In 1180, large-scale civil war broke out in which powerful families competed for control of Japan, using their private armies to fight amongst each other. In 1274 and 1281, the Mongols invaded Japan; even though the Mongols were unsuccessful in both invasions, it cost the Japanese central government a lot of money. The central government had essentially lost all authority, giving more power to the landowners, leaving the emperor as nothing but a figurehead with little actual power.

For nearly 400 years, wealthy landowners, called daimyos, competed for control of Japan, using their private armies of samurai to fight. At any given time, the most powerful landowner, called the shogun, had all the real power in Japan. The shogun maintained control by hiring the best samurai and fighting off the consistent attacks by competing daimyos. During this time period, the Japanese focused on battling for control of their own land against other wealthy families rather than expanding to territories across the sea.

For a while, they continued to trade with other surrounding cultures, but the arrival of Portuguese Christians in 1549 forced Japan to close its doors to trade. Japanese shoguns heard about the fate of Native American civilizations like the Inca and Aztecs. They saw the arrival of Christianity in Japan as a threat to the Japanese way of life, and to the Japanese people themselves.

Japan would remain relatively unchanged in its politics, culture, and way of life until the 1800s, when they gradually re-opened their ports for trade with the outside world, mainly the United States, China, and Europe. It is no coincidence that the feudal society of Japan's Middle Ages began to fade as they opened up their trading ports. By 1868, the feudal society of Japan had all but disappeared, giving more power to the emperor and less power to wealthy landowners.

PART 5

~~~~~

OLD WORLD VS. NEW WORLD

CHAPTER 16

MAYA EMPIRE

Mexico - Central America

250 C.E. to 900 C.E.

~~~~~

As one of the first advanced civilizations to arise in the Americas, the Maya culture set the stage for the development of the region. This advanced society may have collapsed, but its culture lives on through its architecture, and its descendants.

~~~~~

The Yucatan Peninsula features humid, tropical rainforests and relatively flat terrain. It was in this environment that tribes of pre-Maya peoples would unite to form a distinct civilization.

Their civilization was based on a food surplus created from corn, squash, and beans. This food surplus would support a civilization of two million people that occupied more than 40 cities that held populations as high as 50,000 citizens each, making these cities some of the largest urban areas in the world at the time. Their slash-and-burn agricultural methods were eventually transformed into advanced methods of irrigation and terrace farming. With no navigable rivers to facilitate irrigation, Maya farmers had to rely on rainwater and underwater rivers that flowed beneath the limestone bedrock, accessed through cavernous areas called cenotes.

Maya cities features elaborate royal palaces, sacred temples, religious pyramids, and sport courts. Many of the sporting events held on these courts were both culturally and politically significant, with ramifications for both players and supporters. These cities were built out of stone and laid with incredible symmetry and care. In fact, many pyramids were aligned with important astronomical events, like solstices and equinoxes.

Maya religion played center stage in city life; Maya religion worshiped various gods related to nature, which included the gods of the moon, the rain, the sun, and corn. Maya kings were at the top of the social pyramid, claiming that they descended from the gods, acting as mediators between the gods and their subjects. Kings performed major religious ceremonies atop pyramids at the center of massive courtyards that served as community-building events and displays of power.

With religion as a main motivator, the Maya created accurate calendars well into the future based on a 365-day year. They developed mathematics in a way that allowed them to build advanced structures, and they even created the use of the concept of zero.

Though Mayan cities often worked together and shared common cultural features, like language and religion, Mayan city-states frequently fought with each other. As the Maya began to use more and more of their natural resources, resources became increasingly scarce, which caused wars between city-states to increase. Human sacrifices from prisoners of war became more frequent in religious ceremonies. Some of these human sacrifices took place beneath the earth in cenotes, while most occurred in public view atop central pyramids.

Maya religious rituals, cultural features, and written language decoding ciphers were recorded in paper books. As time passed, few of these books survived, largely due to the harsh climates of the rainforest and the violent conquest of Spanish conquistadors. In fact, Spanish conquistadors purposefully burned Maya books as a way to rid the land of any other culture in order to make conquest easier.

Maya civilization declined by about 900 C.E., centuries before the Spanish conquistadors arrived. Historians have not agreed upon a clear reason for the fall of the Maya civilization, though the leading theories include overuse and mismanagement of resources and decades of drought. Some historians conclude that, as resources dwindled, Maya city-states fought with each other in multiple civil wars to compete for these limited resources, which led to their ultimate downfall. Though the Maya civilization crumbled, the descendants of the Maya have lived and thrived in the jungles of Mexico and Guatemala for centuries, continuing on the legacy of Maya culture, language, and art.

CHAPTER 17

INCA EMPIRE

Andes Mountains - South America

1100 C.E. to 1572 C.E.

~~~~~

Creating an advanced society in one of the most dramatic landscapes in the world, the Inca have defied the usual conceptions of how civilizations succeed. Their ruins and culture have permeated the landscape of the Andes Mountains, and the imaginations of historians throughout the world.

~~~~~

The Andes Mountains run along South America's western side. They jump almost immediately upward out of the Pacific Ocean, reaching peaks above 22,000 feet.

This highland territory was home to advanced cultures for thousands of years who acclimated to the highland climate. They used systems of irrigation and terrace farming to build a food surplus of mainly corn and potatoes. Initially, these cultures were organized into a collection of city-states with their own independent governments, social structures, and economies that occasionally traded with one another for resources they needed.

By the 12th century, the Inca people had created a thriving culture in their city-state of Cusco, which sits in a valley with an elevation of 11,000 feet above sea level. As the city-state of Cusco began to grow in strength, it started to conquer neighboring city-states through war. This expanded Cusco's food surplus and cultural influence through the Andes region.

By the early 1400s, Emperor Viracocha Inca dramatically expanded the Inca empire through military power, and stationed military garrisons in each conquered territory to maintain control. During this era of rapid expansion, successive Inca emperors would continue to expand the empire to control territories in modern-day Peru, Chile, Bolivia, and Ecuador, with the center of the Inca Empire remaining in Cusco.

Religious life in Cusco focused on a polytheistic system, with major gods dedicated to the sun, moon, earth, rain, and sky. Religious temples played a major role in ceremonies, like the Temple of the Sun in the center of the city. Inca religious leaders mummified deceased emperors, whose corpses eventually became sacred relics. Oftentimes, these emperors were buried in line with other significant Inca temples and astronomically significant patterns.

Astronomy played a role in Inca religion as well, with temples and buildings aligned with significant star patterns and lunar events. In fact, one of the largest religious festivals, *Inti Raymi*, celebrated the Winter Solstice. In fact, the festival is still celebrated in Cusco in the modern era as a way for people to connect with their ancestry, heritage, and traditional belief system.

Large buildings were constructed in and around the city of Cusco. These buildings were crafted as military defense barracks, government buildings, palaces, and religious temples. These major buildings were created from large stone blocks, though the Inca never used mortar or any substance that glued stones together. Instead, they perfectly crafted each stone to fit seamlessly with the next, so seamlessly that they were watertight. Without the reliance on mortar, the stones were able to move slightly and shift during the many earthquakes that occur in the Andes without breaking down, making buildings strong and timeless. Examples of this can be seen in the modern city of Cusco, where Inca walls still serve as the foundation for many modern buildings.

The legendary city of Machu Picchu is another prime example of Inca ingenuity. Likely built as a royal getaway deep in the Andes Mountains, Machu Picchu sits hidden above the river valley that dives below it. The city contained residences for royalty, religious leaders, and farmers who all moved around the intricate networks of pathways that lined the cliff edges.

With the alpaca being one of the largest animals in the Andes, the Inca never used large animals as beasts of burden. They also never used a wheel. For such an advanced society to create impeccable buildings at 12,000 feet without beasts of burden or the wheel has baffled historians for centuries. The Inca also never developed a written language system, but they did have a recording-keeping system that involved tying knots in a pattern on different colored strings.

The dialect of Quechua became the common language throughout much of the empire, and the language is still spoken in many Andean villages today. Communication between government officials, military garrisons, and everyday citizens was conducted along the 15,000 miles of trails that weaved throughout the empire. Rather than sending messages by written letter, people would send runners who were capable of covering 150 miles per day to deliver verbal messages.

At its peak, the Inca Empire contained over 12 million citizens and over 100 individual ethnic groups. The vast empire began to decline as the Spanish arrived on South America's east coast. Diseases like smallpox brought by Spaniards infiltrated Inca society and decimated its population before the Inca people were even aware of Spanish arrival.

Spanish conquistador Francisco Pizarro invaded the Inca empire in 1532, kidnapping and executing Inca emperor,

Atahualpa before invading and destroying the city of Cusco. The remaining Inca loyalists continued to fight against the Spanish by burrowing deeper into the Andes Mountains. In 1572, Tupac Amaru, the last Inca emperor, led a final push against the Spanish and succumbed to Spanish military strength. Those living in Machu Picchu covered the only entrance to the city with boulders and forest until the city was swallowed by the jungle.

The Spanish destroyed sacred Inca temples and used the stones to build Catholic cathedrals on top of the locations where the temples once stood as a way to erase Inca tradition and supplant Spanish colonial rule firmly. They destroyed Inca buildings and built haciendas over them. They purposefully destroyed any writing or records that detailed Inca's advanced civilization, leaving the only remaining history to be passed down verbally through generations.

In 1911, Hiram Bingham followed Andean guides to Machu Picchu, where he found Andean families living on its ruins, using its terraces for subsistence farming. Bingham publicized his "discovery" of Machu Picchu to the world, which introduced an advanced Inca society to a worldwide population who previously gave the Inca little credit for their advanced civilization.

Since then, damage from Andean earthquakes has destroyed some Spanish colonial churches and houses, revealing the well-constructed Inca ruins underneath that still stand as they did 600 years ago.

Cusco still possesses a strong Inca influence that can be seen in their buildings, clothes, and festivals. And small Andean villages that remained relatively untouched by Spanish colonization still live in a way that reflects the old ways of the Inca.

CHAPTER 18

AZTEC EMPIRE

Mexico - North America

1200 C.E. to 1521 C.E.

~~~~~

As one of the last great civilizations of Mesoamerica, the Aztecs struck awe in the eyes of the city-states they acquired, and into the minds of Spanish conquistadors, whose first encounter with the New World was the world the Aztecs built.

~~~~~

Mesoamerica, as pre-Columbian Mexico and Central America is known, is a geographically diverse area. To the north lies a vast desert that is dotted with lakes and rivers that flow from the highlands of the mountains running down the center. Dense jungles exist to the south in the tropical regions.

In the northern and central regions of Mesoamerica in modern-day Mexico, hundreds of independent city-states existed, each with their own governments and customs, though they traded with each other for resources. However, in the 1100s, resources became slightly scarce, which triggered a competition for control of these resources as a means of survival.

According to Aztec mythology, the Mexica people of northern Mesoamerica followed a vision from a god to seek new land; they would only stop when they saw an eagle perch on a cactus with a snake in its beak. Eventually, they settled in the city of Tenochtitlan, which is modern-day Mexico City, and that vision adorns the modern flag of Mexico.

By the 1200s, an alliance formed between the city-states of Texcoco, Tlacopan, and Tenochtitlan. This alliance defeated the surrounding city-states through a series of wars, and the alliance acquired total control of the region. As the alliance started to gain more and more territory, the Mexica leader of Tenochtitlan began to dominate the empire's alliance, becoming the ultimate leader of what would become the Aztec Empire.

The Aztec Empire continued to grow by conquest, taking over much of northern Mesoamerica, with its capital city remaining in Tenochtitlan. The city was built along the western shores of Lake Texcoco. At its peak in the early 1500s, it boasted a population of over 200,000, making it one of the largest cities in the world at the time. The city itself was built atop flooded fields from Lake Texcoco. A massive pyramid stood in the center of the city, while canals surrounded it outward in symmetrical circles. These canals served as transportation throughout the city, fresh water for hydration, and for irrigation purposes to support the empire's growing population.

The city was built to evoke a sense of awe upon all those who saw it, mainly local leaders of city-states that were subjects to the Aztec emperor. The title of emperor was given to the leader of Tenochtitlan, who ruled as supreme leader over all the cities within Aztec control. Though local leaders still commanded their own city, they were required to pay respect and taxes to the emperor at Tenochtitlan on a regular basis.

Religion throughout the Aztec empire took its lead from the religion of the Mexica people, as well as from traditional Mesoamerican beliefs. As a polytheistic society, Aztec religious leaders conducted ceremonies dedicated to a pantheon of gods representing the sun, moon, war, agriculture, the dead, the springtime, etc. Certain parts of the year were dedicated to the worship of certain gods. The timetable throughout the year in which people were supposed to pray to each god was organized into a calendar system, and this calendar was scientifically accurate.

Aztec priests did practice sacrifices to these gods, and this sometimes included human sacrifice, though not as often as Spanish conquistador journals would lead us to believe. The Olmec, predecessors to the Aztec, practiced human sacrifice, and so did many other civilizations in Central America. The Aztec, however, seemed to incorporate it into religious ritual more than their predecessors did. Sacrifices took place high atop pyramids so the entire crowd could see. Using a flint blade, priests would cut into a live body and pull out the human heart, holding it above their head for the crowd to witness. The purpose of this sacrifice was an offering to the gods for any number of hopes, like rain, a good crop year, or good fortune for a new emperor.

Religion was a regular part of daily life for those within the Aztec empire, as was their designated social class structure. The empire featured a somewhat rigid social system, moving from local rulers to nobles, commoners, peasants, and slaves. Social mobility was difficult, but it did occur.

Throughout the empire, the common language of Nahuatl allowed most people to communicate with one another. A written language was developed, though it mostly included glyphs, or pictograms, rather than phonetic lettering.

At its peak, the Aztec empire controlled as many as 11 million people. Some of these people belonged to groups that the Aztecs had conquered by military force. Through its conquering of neighboring territories, the Aztecs acquired many enemy tribes that longed to seek independence and revenge.

In 1519, when Hernán Cortés arrived on the coast of Mexico from Spain, he exploited the tribal enemies of the

Aztecs to fight with the Spanish. With less than 500 Spanish conquistadors, a multitude of tribal enemies, and the spread of disease, Cortés overthrew the Aztec emperor, Motecuhzoma, signifying the fall of the Aztec empire. Aztec pyramids, buildings, and writing would be purposefully destroyed by the Spanish as a strategy to assert their dominance in the region. Mexico City, named after the original Mexica tribe that came to rule the Aztec Empire, was built atop the ruins of Tenochtitlan.

CHAPTER 19

EUROPEAN RENAISSANCE

Western Europe

1400 C.E. to 1600 C.E.

~~~~~

After nearly 1,000 years, European kingdoms had finally achieved the same level of ingenuity that it saw under Roman control. The rebirth of Europe saw innovations and divisions that would forge the future of not only the continent itself, but the entire world.

~~~~~

The term *Renaissance* means "rebirth"; and in the case of the European Renaissance, it signifies the rebirth of Europe. Since the fall of the Roman Empire in 476, Europe had been engulfed in the Dark Ages, a time when learning and progress halted and, in a lot of ways, regressed from the progress that had been made under the Roman Empire. In Medieval Europe, literacy rates were extremely low, poverty rates were extremely high, and innovation was at a minimum.

Meanwhile, in the Middle East and North Africa, Islamic Empires were ushering in a golden age. Learning, scholarship, and innovation were advancing rapidly within the Islamic Caliphates that championed cultural diffusion, acceptance, and progress. This culture of innovation, however, had not reached Europe.

As Christian Europeans invaded Islamic territory during the Crusades in the 13th century, it brought Europeans into contact with the advancements that had swirled throughout the Middle East for the past 400 years. Much of the scientific advancement that the Europeans had been exposed to in the Middle East went against Catholic Church authority during that era.

In the mid-1300s, the Black Plague hit Europe and killed as many as half of the continent's population. This widespread disaster eroded the church's power and authority in Europe, making room for people to experiment with advancements in science. Catholic monks, priests, and scholars began to find ties between the Catholic Church's teachings and scientific advancement, which encouraged more educated people to experiment with scientific theories in a way that they were not allowed to during the Middle Ages.

The concept of a university had existed in the Middle East for centuries, but the concept began to arise in Europe during the end of the Middle Ages, as Catholic schools began to grow. Literacy rates began to increase as a result of this enhanced education. Monks had been preserving ancient texts for centuries, and now more people could read these ideas, along with the texts that Islamic scholars had created.

Literacy rates would skyrocket after the year 1455, when German inventor Johannes Gutenberg took the Chinese idea for moveable type and created the first printing press in Europe. This allowed writers and publishers to print books in mass quantities. The first book printed in Europe was the Bible, a text which most Europeans had not actually ever read themselves; it had just been read to them by clergy members.

As people read the Bible for themselves, they realized that some of what the church was teaching was not actually in the Bible, such as the selling of indulgences, or buying salvation in the afterlife. This led Martin Luther to post 95 theses on the doors of various German churches, stating the factors that he wanted to change within the Catholic Church. This led to a protest for reformation in the church, spawning various divisions of Protestants to splinter into their own factions of Christianity. This is where divisions like Lutheranism came to exist.

During the Renaissance, artists developed a new fascination with the art and architecture of the ancient world. Since Roman and Greek ruins were literally surrounding European cities, artists sought to learn how these ancient superpowers conducted their artistry. Raphael painted the School of Athens to pay homage to these great thinkers of the ancient world.

Wealthy noble families started funding major art projects as a way to show status. The infamous Medici family of Florence, an Italian city-state, became bankers for the church, which allowed them to acquire immense wealth. The Medicis bankrolled artists that would become the faces of the Italian Renaissance. Donatello became a sculptor that would redefine the skill. Brunelleschi built the dome atop Florence's cathedral, an architectural accomplishment that Europe had not seen since the Roman Empire built the Pantheon.

The Medicis also bankrolled Leonardo da Vinci, who painted works like the Mona Lisa. Da Vinci was a true Renaissance man, meaning he practiced multiple disciplines out of genuine curiosity. He conducted forbidden research about human anatomy on cadavers, and he sketched prototypes for flying machines that have been proven to work. Machiavelli wrote *The Prince* for the Medici family as a guide for leadership, which encouraged leaders to be feared rather than loved.

Galileo, another beneficiary of the Medici family, published his scientific findings that the Earth was not the center of the universe; the sun was. Though this is now commonly accepted in the modern scientific world, the Catholic Church actually placed Galileo under house arrest for publishing his findings because they felt that his theories undermined the authority and teachings of the church, who still controlled much of Europe.

Through bribery and political maneuvers, the Medici family saw multiple family members become Popes, as well as monarchs of France. The family influenced some of the most celebrated achievements of the era, as well as some of the most notorious.

The Catholic Church was the largest landholder and wealthiest organization in Europe during the Middle Ages, and it remained so into the early Renaissance. The Catholic Church used this influence to maintain control over governments throughout the continent, and to enhance its elaborate, elegant, royal image.

The Church bankrolled artists to build elaborate new cathedrals, like St. Peter's Basilica in Rome. Florentine artist and architect Michelangelo used his research to build the dome atop St. Peter's Basilica, which was the center of the Roman Catholic Church. He also sculpted *The David*, which art critics consider the most perfect marble statue of the human form ever created. Michelangelo's crown jewel occurred when he painted the ceiling of the Sistine Chapel. About 12 years into his nearly completed painting, he decided that it was not good enough, so he whitewashed the whole ceiling and started over, completing his masterpiece in about two years. Typical of many Renaissance painting, the mural at the Sistine Chapel depicts famous scenes from the Bible.

The Renaissance also saw major innovations in navigation. For about 800 years, Spain and Portugal were controlled by Islamic Caliphates, meaning they were experiencing the Golden Age of Islam, and they had influence from and access to innovations from the Islamic world. Incredible navigation technology came from the Islamic world, like a usable compass, trade wind research, and accurate maps of the known world. So, it is no coincidence that the Age of European Exploration began in Spain and Portugal.

In 1492, Spanish armies defeated the last Muslim stronghold in southern Spain, and the kingdoms of Castile and Aragon united to form a unified Spain. In the same year, an Italian named Christopher Columbus received funding from Spain to sail west on the Atlantic Ocean; knowing the world is round, he expected to reach Asia, cutting off the time-consuming and expensive overland routes of the Silk Road that led to the riches of trade with Asia. He did not count on two continents being in his way, and he landed in the islands of the Caribbean. These two continents would later be named after Italian explorer Amerigo Vespucci, as they entered Renaissance maps as North and South America.

Spanish and Portuguese explorers and conquistadors would spend the next century trying to explore and conquer the globe. Portuguese explorer Vasco da Gama sailed around the Horn of Africa, opening the route for Portuguese colonists to establish trading posts on the continent. In 1519, Portuguese explorer Ferdinand Magellan set sail with funding from Spain to circumnavigate the globe.

Spanish and Portuguese explorers invaded civilizations in the New World of the Americas, where they would steal resources and bring them back to Europe. This established a new connection between the Old World and the New World that would change the globe forever.

CHAPTER 20

COLUMBIAN EXCHANGE

Europe/Africa to the Americas - Atlantic Ocean

1492 C.E. to Present

~~~~~

After Christopher Columbus connected the Old World and the New World, the entire planet was connected in ways it had never been before. Through this process, cultures and habitats were exchanged in a manner that forever changed the landscape of the globe.

~~~~~

When Christopher Columbus sailed the ocean blue in 1492, he unknowingly united the Old World of Europe, Africa, and Asia, with the New World of North and South America. This unification came to be known as the

Columbian Exchange, named for the person who initiated the contact, and it changed the way that the world would interact forever moving forward. Cultures that had previously never been in contact or knew of each other's existence were now standing face to face, trying to figure each other out.

Columbian Exchange began rather violently. Europeans used guns and steel weapons to intimidate indigenous populations throughout the New World, beginning with Columbus. He enslaved native Caribbean islanders on his quest for gold and riches. He would send indigenous people into the jungle to find gold, and if they came back empty handed, he would chop their hands off as a mechanism to terrify other indigenous people from coming back empty handed as well. Similar brutal practices occurred with conquistadors in South America, and with Hernán Cortés' arrival in Mexico.

Though advanced weapons gave Europeans an edge in war, disease was the most common killer of indigenous peoples. After the Black Plague in Europe in the 1350s, Europeans had developed immunities to leftover diseases, like smallpox and influenza. These diseases were entirely foreign to indigenous Americans, and the diseases decimated entire populations of indigenous cultures; oftentimes, these diseases reached indigenous populations prior to contact with Europeans.

European explorers and conquistadors did not just bring diseases and destruction with them; they brought horses with them as well, and this animal did not exist in the

Americas. The horse would become a favorite mode of transportation in cultures throughout North America, especially in the wide-open grasslands of the Great Plains, where cultures founded increased freedom and mobility in their already-nomadic lifestyle.

Mesoamericans had grown corn, or maize, for thousands of years. Corn began as a small plant, and through centuries of selecting the biggest plants, corn eventually evolved into the size of modern corn. Europeans exported it to Europe as a way to enhance their food surplus.

The same can be said of many other food native to the Americas. Potatoes were a staple crop of Andes Mountain civilizations, and were eventually exported to Europe. Potatoes would become the staple crop of Ireland because potatoes could grow in its damp, harsh climate. Tomatoes, a fruit indigenous to the Americas, would make its way to Italy, where it would become the base for what we now consider to be traditional Italian dishes, like pizza. Pasta, a Chinese creation, and red tomato sauce, are now considered to be quintessential Italian food, even though neither food is native to Europe.

Tobacco, a native crop to both North and South America, became insanely popular in Europe after it was brought to the Old World. The wealthy elite used it as a status symbol because it was expensive to transport and it did not grow well in Europe's temperate climate, which made it a rare commodity.

Europeans also came into contact with coffee and chocolate, plants that indigenous Americans had been consuming casually and ritualistically for centuries. Europeans were also going crazy for sugar, which grew in the tropical regions of Asia.

As Europeans began to set up colonies from land they had stolen from native cultures, they grew crops that European climates could not support, but were widely popular in the Old World. Large plantations of tobacco and cotton emerged in the southern part of North America, while large plantations of sugarcane, coffee, and chocolate sprouted in the tropical regions of South America and the Caribbean.

All of these crops were labor-intensive to produce, but extremely lucrative for plantation owners. Europeans began to use their trade networks in Africa to acquire a labor force. Portuguese and English traders would capture and trade for African slaves on the west coast of Africa. These African captives were loaded onto ships in conditions that were unspeakably terrible; slaves were packed and shackled into ships with essentially no food, water, or sanitation. After the long journey across the Atlantic Ocean, slaves were sold to plantation owners.

Most slave-holding civilizations throughout history used slaves from captives of war, or allowed slaves to gain freedom after a certain amount of time served. The new era of slavery instituted by Europeans created a system in which slaves worked the land for life, and their children were born into slavery, extending the lineage of suffering and hardship.

Plantation owners in the Americas would ship their crops to Europe, where they would fetch a high price. That money was used to fund more slave ships from Europe to Africa to capture more slaves, which made the plantation owners wealthier, and increased the supply of these luxury goods in Europe. Historians refer to this cyclical economic system as Triangular Trade, as it connected three continents in a triangular shipping pattern.

European empires became incredibly wealthy and prosperous during this era at the expense of indigenous civilizations, who ultimately suffered from this new contact. While kingdoms like Spain, Portugal, England, and France brew rich and powerful, civilizations in the Americas, Africa, and South Asia would suffer from disease and stolen resources. The new contact that the Columbian Exchange brought to the world would change the shape of history forever, setting up a new era of imperialism and globalization.

PART 6

~~~~~

THE MODERN WORLD

CHAPTER 21

EUROPEAN IMPERIALISM

Worldwide

1500s C.E. to 1940s C.E.

~~~~~

As Europe emerged from the Renaissance, it began to look outward to gather more resources and push itself even further into the future. As a result, indigenous cultures were trampled and destroyed.

~~~~~

After the process of Columbian Exchange began, European countries and kingdoms became extremely wealthy. They took wealth in the form of precious metals and cash crops like tobacco and sugar, and used that economic prosperity to further advance their wealth.

As European wealth grew, these countries fostered a need to permanently establish systems to take resources and further their wealth. Portugal began by setting up small trading colonies along the African coastline as a way to trade slaves and supplies. Africa was difficult for Europeans to conquer due to dense jungle and deadly disease; Europe's presence remained limited to small trading posts on the coastlines for centuries, despite efforts to make war and one-sided treaties with African civilizations.

Spain and Portugal set up colonies in South America, where they mined for gold and grew tropical cash crops, like sugar, chocolate, and coffee. Unlike Africa, indigenous Americans were not immune to diseases brought over by Europeans, so takeover was relatively easy. In 1494, Spain and Portugal split South America down the middle at the Treaty of Tordesillas as a means to avoid war with each other. Today, Brazilians speak Portuguese while the rest of South America speaks Spanish.

Spain began to lose wealth after gold supplies ran low and after expensive wars with other European kingdoms. Other European kingdoms finally caught on to the navigational technologies of Spanish and Portuguese navigators as well. The Dutch began to pursue colonization around the world, mainly through its ties to the Dutch East India Company: a business that operated jointly with the Dutch government.

In the early 1600s, the Dutch would take over territory in North America, founding the city of New Amsterdam, a walled city that brought wealth as a center for agriculture and trade with indigenous American societies. Eventually, the British would take it over and change the name to New York; where the fortified wall used to stand is now modern-day Wall Street.

In the 1700s, the British began to conquer and control large swaths of territory throughout North America. They founded thirteen colonies off the East Coast of North America, and used those colonies to export timber, cotton, and tobacco back to England for sale. These resources made the British Empire extremely rich and powerful. The British also took over islands in the Caribbean, where the government commissioned pirates to steal from rival Spanish gold ships.

The British took over Australia in 1788, and the continent served as a prison colony for Britain's overpopulated prison system. In 1851, gold was discovered in Australia, which caused a massive migration of people to the continent during the gold rush. In order to keep its wealth in the hands of English people, the British government instituted a system of erasing Aboriginal culture from the continent by taking children away from their tribes and teaching them English culture. This generation came to be known as the Stolen Generation.

Britain took control of India gradually through its connection with the British East India Company until its official takeover in the 1850s. Through its conquests, Britain would become the largest empire of all time.

During the 19th century, Europe evolved during an era called the Industrial Revolution. This era saw major innovations in transportation technology, like the steam engine and the railroad, and military technology like the machine gun. It also saw advancements in medicine with immunization.

The Industrial Revolution hit the United States as well, which gave the new nation innovation and motivation to expand its territory. Through deceit and war, the United States invaded North America from the east as they took land from indigenous cultures in the west, along with lands that France, Spain, and England occupied. During this era of continental expansion, United States government and military policies would target indigenous cultures for eradication, killing millions of native peoples during the genocide. The United States would go on to colonize territories like Hawaii, using military force to suppress native rebels who wanted their stolen land back from American plantation owners.

In the age of the Industrial Revolution, Europeans set their sights on adding more land and resources to their growing empires. Since European powers already occupied colonies in North America, South America, Australia, and Asia, this made Africa the next target for these European powers; they viewed Africa as an unclaimed land.

In 1879, King Leopold of Belgium claimed control of the Congo in Africa. He claimed that his motive was to spread Christianity and to stop the African slave trade. However, his actions told a different story. During Belgium's control of the Congo, Belgian colonists enslaved millions of Congolese people who were literally worked to death acquiring rubber for Belgian businessmen.

The wealth that Belgium acquired from the Congo motivated other European powers to do the same. France claimed territory in Africa. Britain followed shortly after, claiming African territory for themselves. And then Germany did the same, and so on and so forth. This rapid land-grab came to be known as the Scramble for Africa. Within a few years, nearly all of Africa had been claimed and overtaken by European nations. Liberia remained independent, but it was essentially a United States colony at that time. Ethiopia remained the only truly independent nation in Africa.

Europeans had major motivations for expanding their empires into Africa. Africa is the most resource-rich continent on the planet, so European nations were motivated economically to acquire raw materials to increase profit. Political motivations included expanding territory in a competitive nature with other European powers. At the time, it was a commonly held social belief in Europe that Europeans were superior to all other people, and many Europeans believed that it was their duty to "civilize" other cultures outside of Europe. There was also the religious motivation to convert more people to the religion of Christianity.

The competition between European powers trying to control Africa became so intense that, in 1884, fourteen European nations came together at the Berlin Conference to officially divide Africa between them. King Leopold of

Belgium described the arrogant attitude of European Imperialism perfectly when he said "I don't want to miss the chance of getting us a slice of this magnificent African cake." At the Berlin Conference, representatives from these European empires placed a large, blank map of Africa on the wall and carved out territory for each of the nations represented at the conference.

No African leaders were even invited to attend the conference, nor were their opinions considered. European leaders gave no regard to splitting up ethnic groups, linguistic groups, previously aligned cultures, or really anything that African representatives may have wanted. Needless to say, European leaders did not allot any territory for African civilizations.

European powers gained wealth and land at the expense of indigenous civilizations. Millions of indigenous African people were killed through war, overworking, and hunger. Resources went to Europe, which left Africans in more and more poverty.

The legacy of Europe's Scramble for Africa can be seen on even the modern-day map of Africa. Most of the modern continent's political borders have changed little since they were drawn on the wall of the Berlin Conference. Britain's control of South Africa's diamond mines would lead to a system of racial segregation called Apartheid that lasted until the 1990s. Many Africans remain in poverty as a result of European Imperialism.

After World War II, European governments would let go of most of their colonies, partly out of economic necessity, and partly out of pressure from other governments. This era brought independence to places in Africa and throughout the world that had not experienced autonomy in centuries; now they could start the process of rebuilding.

CHAPTER 22

WORLD WAR I

Europe

1914 C.E. to 1918 C.E.

~~~~~

As European powers possessed more and more territory across the globe, tensions in their homelands grew to a boiling point. The entire continent of Europe was engulfed in war, and its impact would affect the entire globe.

~~~~~

World War I, known as the Great War during its own era, impacted the entire development of the 20th century, and it all started with one bullet.

For almost 100 years, European powers had coexisted peacefully as they each acquired territory throughout the world. European empires had grown massive and wealthy at the expense of native populations. After the Berlin Conference in 1884 during the Scramble for Africa, it was evident that tensions between competing powers existed.

By 1914, political tensions began to tear apart Europe's peace. The Ottoman Empire's power was dwindling, as was its control of the Balkan Peninsula in southeastern Europe. Meanwhile, Russia and the Austro-Hungarian Empire were gaining influence in the region, but the two empires were competing European powers that were beginning to lose steam. Minority groups in the Austro-Hungarian Empire attempted to control a large population of Slavs within their borders.

Worried about losing power as an empire, Austria Hungary made a power grab and annexed the Balkan provinces of Bosnia-Herzegovina. Serbia, an independent Balkan nation, was angered by this move because they saw Bosnia as a homeland for Serbian people. Serbia fought to gain control of territory in the Balkans from 1912 to 1913, which continued to threaten Austro-Hungarian power.

In the meantime, a series of secret alliances formed between competing European powers; it seemed that these powers knew war was on the horizon. Russia was angry with German annexation of Russian land after the Franco-Prussian War in 1870, so they entered into an alliance with France. Great Britain also entered into an alliance with

Russia because the British navy now saw competition from the growing German navy.

The Triple Entente of Russia, France, and Great Britain faced off against the alliance between the Central Powers of Germany and the Austro-Hungarian Empire. The possibility that a regional conflict in the Balkans could turn into a full-scale European war grew stronger.

On June 28, 1914, Austrian Archduke Franz Ferdinand traveled to Sarajevo to check out the military forces in Bosnia-Herzegovina. Supported by a Serbian terrorist group called the Black Hand that wanted Serbian national independence, 19-year-old Gavrilo Princip assassinated Archduke Franz Ferdinand while the Archduke was in a motorcade parade through the city.

With its credibility at stake, the Austro-Hungarian Empire needed to appear strong in the face of an assassination of one of its leaders. The possibility of Russian intervention meant that Austria-Hungary needed Germany's help to support its retaliation, which it received. Austria-Hungary declared that Serbia must take steps to right the wrongs of the assassination, so Serbia went to Russia for help. Russia mobilized its army because they thought Germany would use this as an excuse to invade the Balkans. Austria-Hungary declared war against Serbia on July 28, and Germany declared war on Russia shortly after that. Germany attacked Russia's ally, France, through Belgium, and this brought Great Britain into the war.

By the time war broke out, it pitted the Central Powers of primarily Germany, Austria-Hungary, and Turkey against the Allies, which consisted mainly of France, Great Britain, Russia, Italy, Japan, and the United States (who entered the war in 1917 near its end). Most of the fighting occurred on two fronts: the Eastern Front and the Western Front. The Eastern Front ran through Western Russia, while the Western Front consisted of a long line of trenches between Belgium, France, and Germany.

Unlike most previous wars, which saw two armies battling with strict rules in open fields, World War I consisted mainly of trench warfare. Trench warfare meant that two armies dug themselves into deep underground trenches and fought from those trenches, creating little movement in battle lines. Because of trench warfare and the Industrial Revolution, World War I saw the first use of modern weaponry. Projectile bombs and poisonous gases were used by both sides to uproot opposing armies from the trenches. Machine guns were used to stop invading armies from charging through no man's land. Airplanes were used for spying and dropping bombs and propaganda literature on enemy territory, and tanks were used to mow down enemy blockades.

The Eastern Front saw much of the same trench warfare as the famous Western Front; however, the temperatures and conditions were much harsher. After successive wars to secure more territory for its own empire, imperial Russia was financially weak. Though most of Russia's 15 million soldiers were fighting with only one bullet per day, Russia's Czar (a term which comes from the Latin word *Caesar*) insisted that the Russian army kept fighting. As Russian casualties neared two million, Russian soldiers and working class civilians grew more and more angry at the Czar, whose family had controlled Russia for about 300 years as a part of the Romanov Dynasty.

During the middle of the war in 1917, Russia went through a major revolution that would change not only the shape of the war, but the rest of the 20th century. A group called the Bolsheviks, led by Vladimir Lenin, took control of Russia through popular support, and executed the Romanov family. The Bolsheviks would institute a communist government and would lay the foundations for what would become the Soviet Union.

Ultimately, the trench warfare of WWI would result in a stalemate, with the Allies claiming victory. On November 11, 1918, Germany declared defeat by signing the Treaty of Versailles. The Treaty of Versailles placed harsh restrictions on Germany as a form of vengeance for their involvement in the Great War. Germany was expected to pay a ridiculous amount of money in reparations, reduce the size of their military, eliminate their submarines, return lands to winning countries, and to essentially give up their colonies across the world. This created a terrible economic situation for the people of Germany and it set the foundations for the rise of the Nazi Party in the 1930s.

The end of World War I resulted in more than 20 million soldier casualties, and 20 million more soldiers were wounded. The war also spread a major influenza epidemic, impacting millions of civilians.

The stipulations of the Treaty of Versailles, and the crumbled imperial dynasties of Germany, Russia, Austria-Hungary, and Turkey would set the stage for a bigger, more devastating war just two decades later.

CHAPTER 23

WORLD WAR II

Pacific Ocean and Europe

1939 C.E. to 1945 C.E.

~~~~~

The aftermath of World War I created even more tension in Europe and in its colonies across the world. As world powers braced for a more devastating war, colonies looked toward independence.

~~~~~

After World War I, the victorious Allied powers of Great Britain, France, Russia, and the United States placed heavy restrictions on Germany, who they blamed for starting the Great War. These restrictions, including the need to repay Great Britain insane amounts of money, caused Germany's economy to plummet, and their national pride took a big hit. Widespread inflation rates caused dire poverty as unemployment rates hit an all-time high. Quality of life for the average German was growing more terrible by the day.

Many Germans looked for someone to blame for their sinking quality of life, and charismatic leaders emerged with motivational speeches to raise the spirits of German citizens. A World War I veteran named Adolf Hitler gained popular support of the German people and was elected into power based on his ideas of expanding German living space and expelling Jewish people, who he blamed for much of Germany's woes.

Hitler scoffed at the Treaty of Versailles by expanding the German military. He bolstered the German economy through government programs, placing a heavy focus on industry. Hitler eliminated his political competition using extralegal methods and established a secret police force that would capture and dispose of citizens who dared to speak out against him. This solidified Hitler's authoritarian power in Germany. Hitler forged an alliance with the Italian dictator, Benito Mussolini, who had gained power and operated with many of the same governing philosophies as Hitler.

Meanwhile, on the other side of the globe, Japan had been expanding their empire gradually over the last half century. When Emperor Hirohito took the throne in 1926, he enhanced his power as the political and spiritual leader of Japan. The Japanese military invaded Manchuria, and then took over China in a violent siege that targeted hundreds of thousands of civilians.

As Japan began to expand their empire to various Pacific Island territories, Germany looked to expand as well. In 1939, Germany began to annex territory that they had controlled before World War I, and the Allied Powers of France and Britain decided to appease the Germans by refraining from making aggressive maneuvers. Hitler viewed this strategy as a sign of weakness, so the Germans continued their expansion and invaded Poland with a lightning-quick takeover strategy called a Blitzkrieg. War in Europe had officially broken out.

Within a year, Germany conquered and controlled nearly all of Europe, fighting against the Soviet Union on the eastern side and against France and Britain on the western side. In 1940, Japan signed the Tripartite Pact, which created an alliance between Japan, Germany, and Italy; this alliance would come to be known as the Axis Powers.

As Japan continued to invade the Pacific Islands and take more territory in China, the United States placed heavy economic sanctions on them that focused on steel and oil supplies. In 1941, Japan bombed Pearl Harbor, a naval base on the U.S. territory of Hawaii. This maneuver was partly retaliation for economic sanctions, and partly a strategy to force the U.S. to fight a war on two fronts: one against Japan in the Pacific, and one against Germany in Europe. In retaliation to Japan's attack, the U.S. government rounded up any person of Japanese descent on the West Coast and forced them to relocate to internment camps, where they were imprisoned.

In Germany, Adolf Hitler's Nazi government followed through on their mission to expel Jewish people from Europe. Nazi officials rounded up European Jews mainly from Germany, Poland, and Austria and forced them into concentration camps. Much of the operations of these camps were conducted in secret; Jews were forced to work like slaves, and many Jews were systematically killed in gas chambers and through medical experiments. This genocide came to be known as the Holocaust.

Wars of the past operated by unwritten rules that involved refraining from targeting civilians, or non-soldiers, but World War II broke that rule in every way. Through a concept called total war, cities and civilian areas were bombed regularly. Citizens were expected to contribute to the war effort by building weapons, buying war bonds to fund the military, etc.

World War II also saw modern warfare escalate through advanced technology. Airplane technology had advanced rapidly since World War I, so many air-based dogfights occurred, along with the use of airplanes to drop bombs on cities and military bases. German industrial companies, like Bavarian Motor Works (BMW) and Porsche, helped to build advanced airplanes and tanks that aided Nazi Germany's expansion and rapid takeover of Europe.

Battles took place across Europe in open fields and within cities themselves, but European colonies in Africa also saw plenty of action. Fighting on the Eastern Front between Germany and Russia saw frigid winters and rapid death tolls due to the weather and limited rations.

In June of 1944, the Allied forces invaded German-occupied France on D-Day, and continued to push further into German territory. By May of 1945, Russian forces and Western Allies had Germany's capital of Berlin surrounded, marking the end of the war in Europe.

Meanwhile, the war in the Pacific raged on. Japan and the United States were engaged in a battle of island-hopping, where both nations tried to control various islands throughout the Pacific.

By the summer of 1945, the United States had developed the world's first nuclear weapon. As they weighed the benefits and drawbacks of a ground invasion of Japan, the United States ultimately elected to use their new weapon of mass destruction. In August of 1945, the United States dropped two nuclear bombs on Japan, marking the only time nuclear weapons have been used on a population. Prior to the United States' usage of nuclear weapons, the Japanese military was nearly ready to surrender, as Soviet Union forces were invading from the west; the United States likely used their devastating weapons to show the Soviet Union, a rising power, that the U.S. would hold more power after the war ended. Japan swiftly surrendered, marking the end of World War II.

Roughly 80 million people died in World War II, which equated to about three percent of the entire world's population. After tragedy and destruction like this, the world sought to heal itself. In Germany, Nazi war criminals who orchestrated the Holocaust genocide were put on trial in Nuremberg to receive their punishment. The Allies placed heavy sanctions on Japan, which required Japan to eliminate its standing army and Emperor Hirohito to surrender any real power. The United Nations was formed with the objective of maintaining peace through diplomacy among all countries. After so many European Jews were displaced and in need of refuge, the nation of Israel was created as a Jewish nation, occupying part of the nation of Palestine. As European countries found themselves fighting against German and Japanese colonization, they found their own possession of colonies to be hypocritical. As a result, European countries surrendered most of their colonies across the world, and these colonies transitioned into independent nations once again.

Some colonies were not surrendered so easily. British controlled India was extremely valuable for the British economy, and it took the non-violent protests of Mahatma Gandhi and his supporters to finally gain India's independence.

Many African nations that had formerly been under European control were now left with power vacuums, as their traditional leadership systems had been destroyed through imperialism. This caused people to compete for control, and much of that competition ended up causing violence and war that impacted civilians. These effects are still felt in parts of Africa today.

The end of World War II saw the world domination of European powers decline drastically, as most of their economic forces and infrastructure were exhausted from back-to-back wars. Two members of the victorious allied powers, the Soviet Union and the United States, remained mostly untouched by the destruction that plagued Europe and Asia after the war. These two nations would rise to the level of superpowers in the wake of World War II, leading to the tense Cold War competition that defined the second half of the 20th century.

CHAPTER 24

MODERN GLOBALIZATION

Worldwide

1960s to Present

~~~~~

Due to modern technology, our world is now more connected than we ever thought possible. This interconnectedness has enhanced commerce and politics, but it has also created major issues that can only be solved on a global scale.

~~~~~

Since the Industrial Revolution of the mid-1800s, the world has become a more connected place, mainly through advancements in transportation and communication. Innovations in steam power made sea voyages much faster and more direct compared to old methods of sailing. Landscapes that had formerly been divided due to impeding physical features and distance were connected through railroads in the 19th century as well. After the Wright Brothers developed human flight, air travel technology grew rapidly until it became a viable option for quick transportation. The early part of the 20th century also saw the widespread use of the automobile, which replaced the horse as the most-used mode of overland transportation.

Innovation in communication became more efficient during the latter part of the 19th century, and into the 20th century. Alexander Graham Bell's invention of the telephone allowed people to communicate vocally over wire instead of needing to physically travel somewhere. The invention of radio communication allowed governments and media outlets to broadcast messages to large crowds without the need for the crowd to be physically present. Television expanded on that concept, allowing broadcasts to feature a visual image of an event or a message. Both the radio and the television ushered in new media for entertainment purposes as well, which shifted how communities and families interacted with one another.

Then, as the 20th century came to a close, the personal computer entered the homes of many people throughout the world. These personal computers were connected through the internet, which originally used telephone wires to connect digital devices. People could communicate digitally through the internet by sending electronic mailing messages that were delivered instantly rather than over the course of weeks through the postal service. As phones became wireless, email, texting, and information gathering became easier as the smartphone developed and grew in popularity.

Government trade regulations used this wave of connectivity to facilitate trade between countries that were now so connected to each other. Governments began to encourage trade by lowering tariffs and taxes for international trade.

As the 20th century pressed forward, the standard of living in developed countries began to rise, and so did the cost of living. This increased the cost of labor for companies who made goods that developed countries wanted to buy. Companies began to produce their products in less developed countries where the cost of living was cheaper.

Companies could acquire resources from their sources all around the world, and then ship those resources to a factory in a less developed country where they did not have to pay workers as much money to assemble their products. These factories where products were manufactured were usually located near water transportation areas, like ports, so they could be moved easily onto ships. Then, these companies would have ships deliver the completed product to their target market in more developed countries around the world. This entire process was cheaper for companies to use by comparison to producing their entire product in their home developed country.

The journey of the t-shirt exemplifies this model of the global economy. The design of the t-shirt might originate in the offices of a United States fashion company, and the designers of this t-shirt will likely earn a large sum of money simply for their idea. The cotton for the t-shirt might come from Egypt, where it can be purchased cheaply. That cotton is shipped to China, where there is a large population of workers to manufacture the shirt in mass quantities for low wages.

This factory is located near the port, where thousands of shirts are loaded onto a ship aimed for Los Angeles. Once the shirts reach Los Angeles, they are distributed by train and truck to stores across the country, where United States consumers will purchase them for a much higher price than it cost to produce the shirt, which brings in a large profit for that t-shirt company. This type of system has created a global trade network that exists with nearly every product on the market.

As with any trade network, cultural diffusion has occurred through globalization, but now it happens at a more rapid pace. Companies like McDonald's that originated in the United States are now diffused into countries all over the world, and their menus cater to local audiences. Hip-hop, a creative concept that started in the United States, has been absorbed into societies across the globe, reflecting local languages and issues. Indian film styles of Bollywood are now viewed and imitated in film studios across the world. Indian yoga is now practiced in every major city in America. We no longer have to go to China to eat Chinese food; we just need to visit the food cart down the street.

Through this enhanced connectivity, more nations are involved in solving a crisis quickly. As modern technologies become more efficiently produced, they become cheaper, which gives people in less developed countries access to these modern technologies. People have more access to information, which can benefit their worldview, enhance overall education, and develop a new understanding of other cultures.

For example, if something happens in India, people in Honduras can find out about it instantly and empathize with a situation. Humans have access to more efficient contact with other people, which allows us to communicate and receive more input in business, politics, and personal lives across the world.

The United Nations sets an example of global collaboration when it comes to solving world issues through diplomacy. Information about plenty of recent international issues have been dispersed through the internet, which has prompted global help through crowdfunding and rapid transportation of goods to those who need it, and with a speed and efficiency unmatched in any era of human history.

On the flip side, since we are members of a global community, we are now all involved in global issues. An issue that used to affect just a single community now means that the entire world not only knows about it through media, but is affected by that issue in some way. As health standards have risen throughout the world, our population has grown exponentially, leaving less physical space for people to live.

This issue of overpopulation means our world needs to produce more food, but the production of more food may lead to overuse of farmland, as it did with the Maya and Great Zimbabwe. Some governments, like China, have tried to institute a one-child policy to reduce the burden of overpopulation in their own countries. Some governments have yet to address the issue and instead have left civilians in charge of figuring it out on their own, which has created slums and food shortages in some of the world's most overpopulated countries.

With overpopulation and enhanced industry comes the issue of water shortage. With more people consuming water, and more fresh water being used for growing more and more crops, people have less access to water throughout the world. Nearly every major source of fresh water throughout the world is becoming increasingly polluted due to a drive for profit and lack of worldwide environmental laws and industrial standards.

The modern world's reliance on plastics has developed a problem in the oceans. Since plastics are made of oil, they are not biodegradable, and a lot of our plastic waste ends up in the oceans, where it disrupts the ecosystem. Climate change caused by the increasing use of resources is making climates more drastic, which is raising ocean levels and causing crop failure across the world.

More people on the planet means more natural resources are needed to sustain the population. This is causing issues like deforestation in forests and rainforests globally, especially in key places like the Amazon. These forests filter harmful carbon dioxide and produce the world's oxygen supply.

Increased connectivity brings with it a slew of issues surrounding cybersecurity, identity theft, data usage, and financial security. With more people sharing and using interconnected online programs, this issue continues to increase.

Though many countries work to maintain peace through diplomacy, the threat of weapons technology remains. Many countries have worked to limit the creation and stockpiling of nuclear weapons as a means to achieve peace in this new globally connected world, but many world powers still wield nuclear weapons to maintain a dominant global position of power.

Going to war in the modern era is not a simple as it seemed to be in other eras of history. Since our world is so globally connected, a war or natural disaster in one country could impact the economies of countries that are connected to it through a domino effect. And the weapons of the modern world don't just affect soldiers; they impact civilians, the planet, and future generations.

So, whether we like it or not, we live in a globalized society where everyone is somehow connected. People are literally connected through business, digitally connected through the internet, or indirectly connected through the process of globalized production. We're all connected in some way, shape, or form, and it doesn't look like our world is making strides to reduce our interconnectivity. At this point, it's up to us to use this connectivity to write the next chapter of history as we work to form the future.

CONCLUSION

As our society pushes forward into the modern era, we continue to write the story of history. Every day, a current event arises that could become tomorrow's impactful historical event, for better or for worse. Controversial and terrifying news headlines like government elections, worldwide wars, economic crises, disease outbreaks, and freak accidents occupy our news feeds and can cause some of us to be afraid of the world.

But, we also need to remember how many positive current events occur that can one day become an impactful historical event as well: government officials who make ethical decisions for their people, organizations that help people rise out of poverty, major campaigns to help fund disaster relief, and the everyday heroes who work to make our world a better place.

In today's world, we have more access to more information than anyone before us has ever had. It's up to us to use this information to make our world a better place. Our world continues to advance at an exponential pace; the issues of today may produce the solutions of tomorrow, unless we as a society choose to ignore those issues. Will our modern technology and drive for profit be our downfall? Or will we use our resources to make our world a better place for all of its citizens?

As historians and students of history, we can turn to the story of those who have come before us in order to guide us in future decisions. We learn from the mistakes and successes of the past to formulate our own wisdom, our own concept of how to move forward.

From Ancient Sumer, we can learn what humans can accomplish when they work together and innovate. The creation of the first civilization on record was a monumental feat that shaped the course of history. Ancient Sumerians also built civilization by consolidating power through war, and they lost their control in much the same way: the first example of the rise and fall of a civilization.

The Ancient Egyptians gave us widespread agriculture that supported a large population using innovative techniques. They also gave us everlasting monuments, rituals, and mythologies that have found their way into our modern cultures as well. The desire to be remembered like a pharaoh in a pyramid has been the quest of powerful leaders for millennia. On the other hand, much of their power and infrastructure systems were built through a social structure that consolidated absolute power into the hands of one person while suppressing the rights and living conditions of the many. Unfortunately, this concept still permeates societies today.

Recent studies of the Indus River Valley have given historians much excitement and cause for re-examining long-held assumptions about history itself. Through the investigations and archaeological findings of Indus River Valley sites, historians are challenging the longstanding beliefs about where civilization began, who started this movement, and which groups were actually more advanced than others.

Aboriginal Australia provides us with a glimpse into pre-history, a glimpse into a culture that still exists, despite extreme adversity. We can learn to appreciate storytelling, nature, our ancestors, and our elders. We can learn from and appreciate a civilization that has only undergone changes within the recent era. Unfortunately, the lessons we learn from studying modern Aboriginal history shows us the extent to which powerful empires (like Great Britain) will go to extinguish other cultures in order to supplant their own power.

Ancient Greece continues to excite western culture, as it has for centuries. We can understand how overcoming geographic obstacles can lead to certain political and societal trends. By studying Athens, we look into an experiment that championed the will of the people over the rule of one leader; however, in practice, this didn't work out as well as the original democrats had hoped. Though all citizens had the right to vote on any law, the idea of who a citizen fell short of our modern ideals that focus on inclusion (even though this idea of inclusion in citizenship is relatively recent, unfortunately). From Sparta, we learn that a strong military and a mindset of expansion can win territory and resources quickly, but it can also be the downfall of a society.

Roman Republic history teaches us that electing leaders to represent our ideas can make government more efficient, but we also see examples of how this can lead to the abuse of power. Efficiency in government means advanced infrastructure that can benefit even the lowest on the social pyramid, but a powerful government can also use propaganda to sway the opinions of the masses.

The Roman Empire shows us that one person can gain power and influence over a massive territory, and it shows us that expanding territory through military force can be economically lucrative. However, basing an economy on military expansion negatively affects those who are being conquered. And when the conquering stops, the economy slows, the conquered revolt, and even the largest empires can crumble.

Han China gives us insight into how a civilization can last sustainably while still having power consolidation. Through the right government mindset, the most qualified people can help a country, territory, or city using their best skills. And living in an area with valuable, useful natural resources helps. We also find that ruling with cruelty and fear tactics only works for so long before citizens demand change. Through innovation, proper resources, trade, and the removal of ego from government, a society can remain relatively unchanged for centuries.

By looking at the history of the Silk Road, we find the value in trade. We see that societies can have what they need through peace rather than war. We see that trade promotes interactions between different cultures, providing a better understanding of those who may appear different. Ideas spread and are adapted by other societies, making their lives more efficient. But we also see how greed and drive for profit can turn positive motives into nefarious ones, negatively impacting the lives of the most unwitting participants.

Through our studies of the Mali Empire, we find that geographic location and possessing valuable goods can bring people together on a quest for knowledge and intellect. When a nation's wealth is used to better the world and its people, wonderful ideas can arise. But the pride that comes with having great wealth can also bring about one's own downfall.

Great Zimbabwe shows us that trade and interaction can turn a small village into a thriving state. But the mismanagement of resources that comes with a thriving state can cause that state to crumble. It also shows us that an area that American and European historians have so often pushed to the side has actually been thriving and innovating much longer than historians have given them credit for, proving that cultural bias exists heavily in the telling of history.

Medieval Europe tells us that the romanticism of castles, knights, and shining armor was in fact a myth. For a large majority of people, life was probably pretty terrible. We learn that the need for protection in the absence of a centralized government can cause warlords to become cruel, powerful leaders. We also learn that people will subject themselves to harsh conditions in order to have their basic needs of food, water, and shelter met.

The Middle Eastern Caliphates, on the other hand, show us that inclusion and acceptance actually enhance a society intellectually, economically, and technologically. The acceptance of multiple cultures under one government territory produced some of the most advanced thinking and ideas that the world has ever seen. And we see that when creativity and free-thinking intellectuals are suppressed and silenced, a society can crumble quickly.

By studying the Mongol Empire, we see that a strong leader who appoints officials based on merit instead of background can build a strong team, leading to a strong empire. When a leader actively seeks out perspectives of people with different cultural, religious, ethnic, and societal backgrounds, an empire can thrive, innovating in ways that build the people up, thus making the nation stronger. When power is given to those who want power for their own egos, a large empire can fall, leaving a continent in chaos.

Feudal Japan teaches us that competing for resources only brings suffering for the people in the territory, but trading for resources can bring about peace. Those who seek power for their own egos can only hold onto power for so long, especially if the means of grabbing power come from military force instead of the respect of the people. But we also see that advantageous geographic barriers can allow a people to rule themselves rather than allow an outside government to take control.

Our studies of the Maya Empire allow us to gain insight into the complexities of crafting a large society without many resources. But it also lets us know that, by mismanaging our resources, a society can be swallowed. The Maya show us how innovation, technology, and culture can thrive, but it's also an example of what can happen to a thriving society if they grow too quickly without having a strategy for growth.

The Inca Empire shows us how a civilization can thrive without geographic advantages. In the face of some of the world's tallest mountains, without a wheel or written language, the Inca dominated the Andes politically and culturally. The demise of the Inca, unfortunately, shows us how sometimes the interaction between opposing cultures is not peaceful, especially when one side wants wealth and power.

The Aztec Empire teaches us much the same negative lesson. When two cultures interact, sometimes they have motives of curiosity and friendship, while others have motives of greed, power, and control. However, we do see how a civilization can build a strong economy and elaborate urban areas, albeit at the expense of conquering territories themselves.

By exploring the European Renaissance, we see what a culture of inquiry can do for the world. We see how science and religion sometime quarrel, but we also see how religious institutions positively impact the world of art and science. We see what happens when people question authority; sometimes it's dangerous, but sometimes it's necessary. We also see examples of how studying history can lead to further innovation.

Through the Columbian Exchange, we see how different cultures can exchange goods and ideas in ways that positively impact their own cultures. On the flip side, we see how these exchanges can be detrimental to those in disadvantageous situations. We also see how greedy motivations of profit can create systems that place certain people in terrible situations, creating ripple effects further along in history.

The era of European Imperialism furthers this concept. We see how control of land and resources can bring economic prosperity to those who control the land and resources. However, we see what terrible lengths humans can go to acquire more wealth and power for themselves. We also see the impact of political and economic decisions further along in history; unfortunately, the impact of European Imperialism is still felt across the world today in negative ways.

World War I shows us how competition for power can lead to terror and pain. It shows us that the drive for control and influence can lead entire nations to go to war, wars in which those who fight for power are not the ones actually fighting in the trenches. We also see how enacting vengeful tactics in the name of peace can lead to even more animosity down the road.

World War II teaches us valuable lessons on how to treat fellow human beings. We see that technology is not always used for good, and we see that acceptance of those who might be different is not always the norm. We find that when social pressures continue to build, people tend to go along with those pressures for fear of being ostracized. And, unfortunately, we see that nations use propaganda and lies to get their civilians to support what they're doing, no matter how evil those choices might be.

Modern Globalization shows us where we are. It shows us that technology can connect far-reaching societies and increase lifespans. It also shows us that with more people comes more issues that need solving. We also see commonalities with issues that other historical eras had to wrestle with: resource management, roles and responsibilities of governments, and the spread of ideas used for both good and bad. We also know that this is the era that we are currently in the process of shaping.

When we reflect on the cultures and eras that have come before us, we often scoff at the missteps that some of those leaders and societies made. How could Medieval Europeans have thought the Earth was the center of the Universe? How could the Maya have overused all of their resources to the point of destruction? Why did the Chinese close their ports to trade when the Silk Road was booming? How could there have been so much religious and cultural intolerance between European Christians and Middle Eastern Muslims that a war was fought over it? People in the future could very well ask those same questions about us. In our modern era, we make mistakes that future generations may, and probably will, laugh at.

But, we are probably doing a lot of things the right way, just as many civilizations of the past did as well. The Roman Empire provided fresh running water to even the poorest of its citizens. Islamic Caliphates were tolerant of other religions. The Mongols provided public education to its people. Merchants along the Silk Road traded with and interacted with people who didn't look like them, speak like them, or believe the same things as them, but they still interacted with civility and respect. In a lot of ways, our modern world has adopted some of these lessons for our own purposes.

We live in our own era of history, just like the Mongols lived in their own. Our current events will become tomorrow's historical events from which future generations will learn. Sometimes we read about history as if it happened to people who were not like us, didn't have the same feelings or fears as us. But, the figures, cultures, and civilizations were a lot like us. They had similar thoughts, needs, wants, fears, and successes. We're living in history just as the Mongols were living in theirs. In 400 years, how will we be remembered? What will people write about our society in the history books? Will we be remembered for our forward-thinking vision, our inclusion, and our dedication to our citizens? Or will we be remembered for our hunger for power, riches, and territory?

One of the main purposes of studying history is to learn from the past. By learning about the successes of those who existed in the chapters before us, we can build on those successes and shape a better future for those who come in the chapters ahead. By learning from the failures and the missteps of the past, we can make a conscious effort to leave those mistakes in the past as to not repeat them for future generations.

Each generation has its successes, and each generation has its regrets. As our world grows even more intertwined and complex, it is imperative that we learn from past generations in order to create a more successful, peaceful, and harmonious world. It's up to us to shape where the world goes from here. Now. In this pivotal time in history. It's up to us to write our own future. As we continue to write the story of the world, it's up to us as its authors to craft the next chapter.

SELECT BIBLIOGRAPHY

Beard, Mary. *SPQR: a History of Ancient Rome*. Profile Books, 2016. Beard illustrates the power and audacity of the Roman Empire, dedicating each chapter to a specific emperor or influential figure who shaped the course of the empire. She conveys details from the transition of Roman government from a republic to an empire, and finishes her analysis and storytelling with the downfall of the empire itself. This source provided expert insight into the operations, beliefs, and customs of the Roman Empire, dealing with average people, slaves, women, soldiers, and male politicians.

Bower, Bert, and Jim Lobdell. *History Alive!: The Medieval World and beyond*. Palo Alto, CA: Teachers' Curriculum Institute, 2005. The authors provide a well-constructed albeit surface-level description of major cultures, eras, and civilizations throughout the medieval world. This source provided starting points for the studies of Medieval Europe, Middle Eastern Caliphates, the Mongol Empire, and ancient civilizations from which to base further research. It covers basic religious, economic, political, geographic, and historical concepts from the major medieval regions, using a mostly traditional narrative to write the story, though it does incorporate a more modern take on certain civilizations that had once been overlooked or underappreciated by western historians.

Buruma, Ian. *Year Zero: A History of 1945.* New York, NY: Penguin Books, 2014. In this compelling history of 1945, Buruma discusses how the world rebuilt itself after the destruction of World War II. The author briefly describes the causes and timeline of the war from both the Pacific and in Europe; however, the bulk of the work discusses the aftermath of the war across Europe and the Pacific. It deals with how certain countries consolidated power while other former powers lost control It wrestles with the issues of former colonies gaining independence while former powers still tried to exert indirect influence. It discusses how the victors sought justice for war crimes against enemy countries, both in legal courts and at the civilian level. And the work discusses how the destroyed countries planned to rebuild their economies after the devastating effects of the war.

Chasteen, John Charles. *Born in Blood and Fire: Latin American Voices.* W.W. Norton and Company, 2018. This book traces the history of Latin America, starting with the arrival of Christopher Columbus in 1492. This history deals with the cultures that existed in Latin America at the point of Columbian Exchange, and it follows their clashes with European powers. It wrestles with Columbian Exchange and European imperialism until the modern era, in which it traces the various revolutions and gains for independence made by former colonial territories.

Diamond, Jared M. *Collapse: How Societies Choose to Fail or Succeed.* Revised ed. New York, NY: Penguin, 2011. Expertly researched, this work discusses once-thriving civilizations, and it details various theories as to how those societies fell apart. It draws parallels between many of these societies and their ultimate downfalls, which include major issues such as resource mismanagement, overpopulation, and poor leadership foundations, along with expansion mindsets that caused backlash. Serving as a flagship source for this work, Diamond details societies like the Maya, China, Central Africa, Australia, Easter Island, Viking territory, and the modern world, connecting all of these eras through the inevitable collapses that occurred and the common reasons between all of those societies for their collapses.

Diamond, Jared M. *Guns, Germs, and Steel: The Fates of Human Societies.* New York, NY: W.W. Norton & Company, 2017. This work details various theories as to why certain societies conquered and controlled other societies. Diamond expertly researches and lays out these theories, which boil down to three main reasons for the militaristic and technological success of some societies over others: the development of guns, exposure over centuries to certain diseases that produced immunities, and access to resources and technologies to make steel. Civilizations in Mesopotamia created a food surplus system that allowed interconnectivity between Europe and Asia, which, through cultural diffusion, brought diseases, gunpowder, and metalworking technologies to a society that had little resources (Europe). This drive for resources paired with superior technology and immunity to diseases (both of which occurred simply because of the luck of their geographic location) and it allowed Europeans to take over most of the world during the second half of the last millennium.

Foer, Franklin. *How Soccer Explains the World: an Unlikely Theory of Globalization.* Harper Perennial, 2010. The author explores globalization, using soccer as a vehicle to explain the impact of globalization around the modern world. This work deals with economic, political, religious, and geographic influences that globalization has on countries like Spain, Russia, and Saudi Arabia. With examples detailing revolutionary expression, religious influence, and political corruption, Foer masterfully weaves a narrative of globalization through the lens of soccer and global sport.

Frey, Wendy, John Bergez, and Amy Joseph. *History Alive!: The Ancient World.* Palo Alto, CA: Teachers' Curriculum Institute, 2011. This work details the rise of civilizations in the ancient world, specifically working with Ancient Egypt, Mesopotamia, Indus River Valley, Rome, China, and Greece. This work served as a foundation for basic understanding of these civilizations, discussing political, geographic, economic, cultural, and religious concepts at a surface level. It does feature a traditional western perspective on these particular eras, though it does incorporate modern research as well.

Gates, Henry Louis, et al. *Africa's Great Civilizations*, Season 1, episode 1-6, Public Broadcasting Service, 2017. Gates details the history of Africa in this groundbreaking series that uses previously ignored research to weave the tale of the continent. Gates focuses on ancient civilizations that constructed some of the ancient world's most technologically and socially sophisticated cultures. He discusses the intricate trade networks that African societies fueled, further exploring Africa's central connection points to other places through the medieval world. He explores the art, architecture, literature, religions, governments, and social structures that made Africa a thriving continent for millennia. And he discusses the modern era, detailing how Africa's interactions with Europe fueled a slave trade that severely damaged the continent.

Gould, Ben, et al. *Mankind: The Story of All of Us*, Season 1, episode 1-12, History Channel, 2012. This documentary series attempts to tell the story of humanity in 12 episodes, focusing on the evolution of humans into the modern era. This series used dramatic reenactments and expert analysis to relay the journey of humans out of Africa, the rise of civilizations, the details of major civilizations, and the technologies that shaped our world into what it is today. Though some major eras and civilizations are excluded, this documentary series developed a compelling narrative that served as a baseline for the story of humanity from a social and technological perspective.

Kurlansky, Mark. *Salt: A World History*. New York, NY: Penguin Putnam, 2002. This work details the history of the world through the lens of one of its most historically valuable commodities: salt. The author traces salt's origins as a commodity in the ancient world through the modern day, also detailing major innovations, societies, and trade routes that have arisen as a result of this commodity's trade. The work moves through the ancient world, to ancient China, to Africa, to Europe, to modern North America, showcasing the innovation, greed, and influence that this seemingly common commodity has had on world history. The work served as a major influence for this work during the Han China, Mali Empire, Silk Road, Columbian Exchange, and European Imperialism sections, servings as a well-researched source for economics and natural resources, along with trade and exchange that occurred during these particular eras.

Machiavelli, Niccolo. *The Prince.* Translated by W. K. Marriott, Ann Arbor Media Group, 2009. This classic work was written for the Medici family of Florence as a guide for how to rule effectively. Written in 1532, this work draws the conclusion that a leader who generates fear in his subjects will have a stronger control on society than one who acquires the love of the people. This principle served as a guideline for how European rules governed throughout Europe's rise out of the Middle Ages and into Europe's imperial era. The work's impact on modern government makes this work an integral part of understanding our society today, and it's the reason that this work is still studied in modern education systems.

Mann, Charles C. *1491: New Revelations of the Americas before Columbus.* New York: Knopf, 2006. The author uses expert research to detail what North and South

America looked like before the arrival of Columbus and the influences that came along with Columbian Exchange. This work served as a basis for understanding the Inca, Aztec, Maya, and Columbian Exchange sections, determining the continents' populations, demographics, cultures, religions, agricultural practices, and social structures. Without this work, traditional narratives of indigenous cultures in the Americas would still thrive in western historical dialogue; this work has shifted the conversation and the focus of the history of the Americas before the arrival of Columbus.

Mann, Charles C. *1493: Uncovering the New World Columbus Created*. New York, NY: Alfred A. Knopf, 2011. As a follow-up to *1491*, this work traces the impact of Columbian Exchange on North and South America, as well as its influence on Europe, Asia, and Africa. It takes an approach based on agriculture and vegetation, but it weaves in understandings about how societies and cultures were impacted as a result of these changes and shifts. As goods and people moved between the Old World and the New World, societies adapted and changed in ways that they never have before, and likely never will again, due to the complete unfamiliarity between both parts of the world until the fateful year of 1492, when two worlds collided and set in motion the largest instance of cultural diffusion that has ever occurred.

Mansfield, Peter. *A History of the Middle East.* Edited by
Nicolas Pelham, Penguin Books, 2019. The author
discusses the history of the Middle East region from a
religious, cultural, and political perspective. This work
utilizes expert research to detail the rise of Islamic
caliphates during the medieval era, along with the fall
of those civilizations. It also focuses on the modern
world through its investigation of European imperialism's impact on the region, an influence that
seems to be the cause of many of the issues that plague
the region during the modern era. The work also
focuses heavily on economics as a main motivator for
medieval rulers, colonial powers, and modern
businesses to control the area's valuable resources. It
also focuses on the area's central location between
Asia, Africa, and Europe, leading to the diverse
demographics and intense cultural diffusion that
occurred and still occurs in the crossroads of the
Middle East.

Polo, Marco. *The Travels of Marco Polo.* Translated by Milton
Allan Rugoff, The New American Library, Inc., 1961.
This classic travel journal details Marco Polo's journey
from Italy to Mongol-controlled China. Though many
historians are skeptical of Polo's accuracy, the journal
describes in great detail Kublai Khan's court, the inner
workings of Mongolian and Chinese society, and the
intricate trade routes that the Mongol rulers

established. Whether or not some specific details (or the whole journey) are accurate or fabricated, it serves as a guide for what Europeans thought about the East, and what Europeans of the pre-Renaissance era valued as important in another society and in their own.

Weatherford, Jack. *Genghis Khan and the Making of the Modern World*. New York, NY: Three Rivers Press, 2012. This work focuses on the history Genghis Khan, who united the tribes of the Mongolian Steppe to take over the largest contiguous empire in history. The work emphasizes the traditional narrative of Genghis Khan, including the terror and bloodshed, but it also weaves a different narrative, a story that portrays Genghis Khan as tolerant of other cultures, innovative in his treatment of civilians, and innovative in his strategies for governing. This work is based heavily on the *Secret History of the Mongols*, which was written by Genghis Khan's relatives and successors, so some of the details may have bias, but it also features evidence from other medieval works written throughout the massive expanse that was the Mongol Empire.

Stone, Oliver, director. *Oliver Stone's Untold History of the United States*. Ixtlan Productions, Showtime Productions, 2012. This documentary series charts the history of the United States during the late-19th and 20th centuries. It uses heavy bias (albeit acknowledged bias), focusing its emphasis on factors in U.S. history that are not part of the traditional narrative. Stone portrays the U.S. as an imperial power that took advantage of the decline of European powers during the tumultuous 20th century, using its influence to create a powerful government, economy, and global presence that went essentially unchecked. Though the documentary series is biased, it does bring up major issues that plagued the world during the era of European imperialism, the world wars, and still plague our modern world as we move through this period of modern globalization.

ACKNOWLEDGMENTS

First and foremost, I want to thank my family for allowing me to take time to read, research, and write about history. To my wife, thank you for listening to me as I drone on about what I deem to be exciting revelations about history; thanks for humoring me. You inspire and encourage me to be the best version of myself, and to explore the things that I'm passionate about. Thank you for your support; I love you.

Next, I want to thank my colleagues who encourage me to learn as much as I can about everything that I can. You consistently share new findings that you've uncovered, and you humor me when I share my findings too. You all push me to be a better educator every single day. Your dedication to the craft is incredible, and I wouldn't be able to impact students if it wasn't for your guidance and honesty. Thank you!

I need to thank my students, who ask thought-provoking questions that lead us to explore history even further. Your curiosity about the world and the people in it make teaching so much fun. You push me to learn new things by the questions that you ask, and you inspire me to keep on learning more so that I can continue to teach to the best of my abilities. You all have such bright futures, and you understand that learning about the past is a way to shape your own future for the better.

And, of course, I want to thank my parents for instilling within me a love for writing, a capacity for adventure, and a desire to explore and understand the world. Thank you for providing me with opportunities to grow and for helping me when I faltered. Thank you for your inspiration, example, and unconditional love. Thanks to my siblings for encouraging me to be courageous in the face of potential failure, and to be confident in what I want to do.

I want to thank those authors, directors, and researchers who I learned from, and for those who produced work that gave me the necessary information to produce this work. You all do (and have done) such important work in the field of history, and it's because of you that the narrative of history is consistently moving toward becoming more accurate, more wholistic, and more equal. Keep doing what you're doing so you can inspire the next generation to take over where you leave off.

Lastly, I'd like to thank my former teachers; you instilled in me a love of history, a respect for people, and a curiosity about culture that led me down this path. Thank you for inspiring me, even when you didn't know you were doing so. Thank you for educating me and teaching me about the world, and the places and people in it. It's because of people like you that people like me even get to read, research, and write about our passions in the first place. Thank you for your patience, your guidance, and your kindness; you've truly changed lives!

ABOUT THE AUTHOR

Tom Malone was born and raised in Portland, Oregon, where he developed a passion for the history and culture of the city. And rain and coffee. He earned his bachelor's degree in history, journalism, and Spanish at the University of Oregon, and he earned his master's degree in education at the University of Portland. Currently, Malone teaches history and English at the secondary level near Denver, Colorado.

Malone explores the world as much as possible. His recent adventures include: backpacking through the Andes Mountains in Peru, road-tripping through Ireland, and scuba diving in Jamaica. He has spent time in the jungles of Honduras, and time in Spain studying the country's history and language. Living at the base of the Rocky Mountains, Malone snowboards every winter and goes fishing every summer. Oh yeah, and he reads and writes a lot.

OTHER WORKS BY AUTHOR

Across Americana: A Novel

In the Shadow of the Spanish Sun

Sloan Fitzpatrick: Middle School Journalist